To Be Made Whole:

A Handbook for Inner Healing

By Pastor Jim Hill

JIM HILL

To Be Made Whole

By Pastor Jim Hill

Copyright © 2007 by Jim Hill

The North Clairemont United Methodist Church

4570 Mt. Herbert Avenue

San Diego, California 92117

Printed in the United States of America

ISBN 1-931178-16-X

All rights reserved solely by the author. The author guarantees all contents are original and do not infringe upon the legal rights of any other person or work. No part of this book may be reproduced in any form without the permission of the author. The views expressed in this book are not necessarily those of the publisher.

Table of Contents

Commendations v

Foreword My Road to Discovery of Spiritual Healing ...ix

Chapter One: Introductory Examples of Healing
   by Spiritual Means 1

Chapter Two: The Law of Cause and Effect
   Has Not Been Repealed, or Effects Have Causes
   And It's Okay to Look for Them 17

Chapter Three: If You Live in the State of Denial, Move 35

Chapter Four: How to Use This Stuff 47

Chapter Five: We Need Not Just Godly Principles,
   But God 71

Chapter Six: Mourning Is God's Road to Comfort 77

Chapter Seven: Forgiveness is the Road to Freedom 91

Chapter Eight: Repentance Is a Good Thing: It's a
   Do-Over 105

Chapter Nine: Re-program Your Understanding 125

Chapter Ten: You've Got to Ask 149

Chapter Eleven: God Did Not Abandon You 161

A Final Word of Encouragement 173

About the Author 179

JIM HILL

Commendations:

Pastors, laity, and counselors will appreciate Pastor Jim Hill's journey & discoveries in spiritual healing. His presentation is true to the reality of God and is in harmony with effective psychological principles that by necessity must also rely on true principles. His conversational style of writing is engaging and very user friendly. The sincere seeker of healing and peace will appreciate the results of applying God's principles in Truth and Grace and I pray achieve a deeper or possibly new relationship with Jesus Christ.

Dr. Mel Estey, Captain USN Ret.,
Psychologist at Donovan State Prison

Jim, your book is great! Great insights for both the layperson and other pastors. Easy to read. Your love and compassion for people shines thru with every word. May God bless this book and you.

Karen J. Lenell, MA, MFT
Marriage and Family Therapist with Family Consultation Service

Many thought the heyday of "inner healing" had passed, but Jim Hill reminds us that this is not so. In fact, he persuasively reclaims the promise of healing for the wounds and crises of life has never been lost. The uniqueness of Hill's testimony is two fold: first, he writes with the voice of experience - inner healing has been a part of his ministry for many years. He knows the promises of Christ are still available. Second, he buttresses his convictions with sound theology. Those who minister in this way can trust his thinking. He knows the faith and trusts it. This is no fly by night guide - It is here to stay. Read it with assurance.

Rev. Dr. H. Newton Malony, Ph.D.,
Professor of Psychology
School of Psychology at Fuller Theological Seminary

    I doubt seriously if Pastor Hill would call himself a healer. In fact, over the last 20 years or so, many wonderful healings, emotional and physical have occurred through his personal ministry and at the church he shepherds. At all times, he would attribute good being done to the wonderful grace and power of God the Holy Spirit, accomplished by the authority of Christ. But a healer, no, a servant, definitely. Yet, not just any servant, but one whom through personal healing, much agonizing study, success and failure, and practice has seen and continues to see miraculous and overtime healing and restoration of the broken in mind, body and spirit.

    What Pastor Hill has learned has been, condensed to the book you have in your hands. Illustrated here are the testimonies of some of the struggling saints of God who have experience God's mercy and grace to heal, and provided are the principles of healing and specific processes that have proven helpful in practical, hands on ministry.

Thus, I commend this book to you. In fact, we have decided to add it to our required reading for our counseling students studying inner healing, and highly recommend it for anyone serious about seeing the body of Christ healed and strengthened for the journey of life.

Stan DeKoven, Ph.D.
President
Vision International University

JIM HILL

Foreword
My Road to Discovery of Spiritual Healing

"And as many as touched him were made whole."
– Mark 6:56

I want to speak a little of my personal journey of understanding in this area of healing in the hope that I might, in some small measure, bring the reader along with me on a similar journey. Our culture has been steeped in naturalism or materialism for so long that it is difficult for many to readily give any credence to arguments for godly intervention in the physical realm, and that is precisely what I argue for. Strictly speaking, it is not necessary to read this foreword in order to consider the validity of the arguments I shall present for the principles I offer regarding the healing of a wounded spirit. The principles I shall offer will either rise or fall upon the evidence I marshal for each one in its own place. However, I felt it might serve at least two purposes to give some little testimony about my coming to faith and my experience of divine healing. One purpose is simply that of pleasure. Personally, I always delight to hear reasonably honest testimonies of a person's life or growth in Christ, and I suspect that others who know Jesus enjoy testimonies too. The second purpose relates to my desire to speak to Christianity's "cultured despisers," some of whom, I suspect, now call themselves members of various churches, while many others know full well that they are not in relationship with God. I suspect that there is a readiness to dismiss the examples I have given and the principles I shall speak of on the part of those who have had the misfortune of a "good education" they have not yet been able to overcome. We in the western world have been taught anti-supernaturalism for many decades; indeed, in some regards, it could be said for two or three centuries. This heavy indoctrination in the dogma, currently regnant in our intellectual elites and their subordinate educational institutions, of anti-supernaturalism, or naturalism or materialism, has the unfortunate effect of greatly impeding the ability of its adherents to hear or see truth which does not fit their ideology. By telling you some of my story, you may discover that I really do not have horns and that I am not all that wild and woolly a fellow, which may serve to make it easier for some readers to receive the things that follow. To those ends, I share these next few pages.

It is true that my family went to church when I was young – some. But before long I was far the more devoted a participant. Besides, we were Methodists, and in recent decades, in my part of the country, that has more readily meant a moral earnestness than any real intimacy with God. We might pray for God to help us endure difficulty honorably, but we did not pray for God to change anything. We did not expect that. We were in no way "holy rollers." My family pooh-poohed Billy Graham. (Realize that I am speaking of the 1950's now, and he may have been less mainstream then.) I went to youth group in junior high school years in order to have a parentally acceptable way to get out of the house, but by high school years, I felt very close to God. My faith was ignorant, but very intimate. My youth pastor gave me Rudolph Bultmann's *Kerygma and Myth* to read during high school. Fortunately, I did not understand it.

I started college at Occidental College in Los Angeles, a small, liberal arts college of some repute, founded by Presbyterians about a century ago. It still had required Bible survey courses and a fairly large religion department, filled with ordained ministers who also had PhD's. I was taught that the Bible was written by J, E, D and P, or various editorial schools in some sort of antiquity. Apparently, Moses had very little to do with it, and God even less. Then I took a course called "Current Trends in Christian Thought." In that class we studied Bultmann, Buber, Tillich, Daniel Day Williams, Niebhur, and John A. T. Robinson. Fundamentally, we were taught that the Bible was a book of fairy tales, expressing profound human truths, mind you, but, once again, God had very little to do with it.

Paul Tillich's *Dynamics of Faith* was used to try to justify using Christian language while not meaning anything by it. "Signs" were ordinary words, and they meant what they meant; but "symbols" were super-words, and they changed their meaning only slowly. Therefore, us clever ones could speak of "resurrection" and "God" and "Holy Spirit," and not mean at all what people thought we meant by it – because those words were "symbols," and they changed their meaning only slowly, and we would need to give the less clever people in the pews time to catch up to "us." Well, I thought that was rank dishonesty, and I still do. However, all my teachers said this, and they were ordained ministers and PhD's, and the book jackets on the books they gave us to read said these were the best books in the field, and I was too green at 18 and 19 to know that all book jackets said that about their contents, and, come to think of it, my youth minister when I was in high school gave me one of these books to read too. So, I concluded, it must be that everybody who is educated knows that there really isn't any God. That was quite a shame, but if that's the way it was, well, then that's the way it was. No crutches for me; I'll get along without God. But no lying, please; I'm not going to go to church and use words I don't believe. So I left church.

While hardly the wildest child of my age, I was a young man of my time and place. I tried, with whatever awkwardness or grace I could manage, to sample the sources of meaning offered to me by my culture: wine, women, song and intellectual snobbery. Among other things, I took *The New York Review of Books*, *TLS*, and a variety of other literary, political and general publications, and, later, various academic journals relating to East Asian history, which latter was once my field of study. I have subscribed to dozens of other publications of various sorts over the years and still take more than a dozen, but these are noted to support my claim that I was thoroughly infected with the viewpoint of the academic culture and I was *not* very pious or credulous or inclined to believe in supernatural things for a number of years.

    I became a graduate student in history at UCLA. I went to the cinema only to see "art" films (Bergman, Bunuel, Fellini, Truffaut, Jean Luc Goddard, and so on), until I got sick of them and started to go see Dirty Harry movies, but that was later. I used to give away copies of *The Way of All Flesh* by Butler and Fraser's *The Golden Bough* as reflections of my "evangelization" of folks to the non-theistic estheticism into which I had fallen. Consequently, if I now affirm the existence of God and the reality of healing in the name of Jesus Christ, which I do, it is not because I am merely parroting some myths I learned in childhood. There are reasons why I got to where I am, and I am quite comfortable arguing them with any who think they can seriously challenge my current beliefs. From 1964 to 1978, I did not consider myself a Christian or a theist.

After a few years in my new wilderness, however, I did start going back to church. I went about thirty Sundays out of fifty. I went more "religiously" to brunch at Woody and Eddys' or at the Huntington Sheraton (nice restaurants in Pasadena), but still I went to church most Sundays. I cursed the traffic on the way to church, and recognized the irony of it, but I went. I scammed on the woman three pews in front of me, in my mind, but I went.

I went to a big church to hide. I was afraid if I went to a small church someone would ask me what I was doing there, and I did not know. I went to the First United Methodist Church of Pasadena. This was a wise choice: There was no danger of anyone talking to me there. (Bless his heart, Lambert Baker did come by and chat with me once in a while, which was probably all I was ready for anyway.) If a certain man on staff was going to pray, I would stick my fingers in my ears and make quiet droning noises: It was enough to block out my ability to hear him without bothering anyone else nearby.

I just did not believe him. Since I was not a member, I did not receive their newsletter and did not know when the senior minister would be gone. If this man were going to preach, I got up and left. I had some other, now amusing, disappointments there, but I went. I was looking for something, and I sensed just enough to keep on looking.

Finally, I found two men who seemed to be honest and seemed to believe in something. I began talking with them. They liked the Bible, and I wanted to be their friend, so I decided to read the Bible. Then I found myself moved at certain points. I dismissed it. This, I told myself, was just the stirring of emotions from childhood memories of Christmas pageants and such, nothing more. But eventually it became too much to dismiss. It was never when I had it in mind. I had read this book before, and there were times I told myself that I was going to get zapped at a certain point, but it never happened when I said it would. It always caught me by surprise. There were times when I had not settled in to my reading and I was still in a haze and could not have told you what I was reading if you had asked me, and I would be moved.

When I looked at the meaning of the passages wherein I was moved, I found it was always on something affirming the existence of God and the deity of Christ – the very questions I had at that time. Additionally, C. S. Lewis, Wolfhart Pannenberg and a host of other authors began to give me the intellectual justification for faith that I had needed, but did not have, back in my sophomore year at college. At this point, I would happily argue the rational grounds for faith with anyone seriously interested in the matter. [If the reader is interested, I would now recommend *Miracles* and *Mere Christianity* by C. S. Lewis, *Know Why You Believe* by Paul Little, and *The Case for Faith* and *The Case for Christ* by Lee Strobel and *What Does Anybody Need God For, Anyway?* by Jim Hill for an introduction to the reasonableness of Christian faith.] Leaving out a number of little tidbits perhaps only interesting to me, by the end of 1978, I accepted Jesus Christ as my Lord and Savior, and I was baptized in a mountain stream at first water along the Mount Wilson trail, above Sierra Madre, in November of 1978, and the next Sunday I joined the church I had been attending for six years.

That gets me to some sort of faith, but what about faith for healing? How did that happen? Well, the young evangelical guys who were my new mentors seemed to believe in a God who could do such things. So, I sort of believed too, but I had not seen anything. In 1981, I began to work at that church I had joined as Lay Director of Evangelism. I saw many things then, changed lives and new joy, but nothing on the healing front. That came with my next church.

Having concluded that God was calling me into ordained ministry late in 1978, rather against my will since I did not really want to be one of those guys who had disappointed me, I began the ordination process. I was ordained in 1984, finished seminary in 1985, and went to pastor the First United Methodist Church of Highland in June of 1985. My predecessor had left the church months before to start his own church in the area. There were many problems and many problems overcome, but only a few of them relate to my theme.

Among the things I did there was to start an evening service. I know I was merely aping the pattern I had seen at a vastly larger church I had visited, and building the service did not make them come, but I still liked the idea. A parishioner of mine asked that I invite to speak at the Evening Service a man he knew who had a healing ministry. Well, why not? You have an Evening Service, in part, just to have a place to take risks without risking the displeasure of your whole congregation. So I invited him. He was more rotund than I have ever been, and I no longer cut the figure I should like. He was a bit rumpled. He looked like he might fit well in a tent and with sawdust on the floor. He spoke a little loudly for me, and he simply was not my ideal for a minister. (Remember that I was still a bit snobby.) However, he did have one virtue that many ministers do not appear to have: He knew God.

He spoke on healing. Then he asked if anyone had a pain, so that he could pray for it to go, and thus illustrate God's healing. No one volunteered. Well, a pastor is always concerned that his programs go well, and I did have a little pain, and no one else was volunteering, so I volunteered.

In 1968, I had been crossing a street in Venice (California, not Italy). I looked north and saw a bus was stopped, I looked south and saw traffic was far enough away for me to cross, and I went into the street. What I did not realize was that the bus to my north was not stopped for the light, but to take on passengers, and on the other side of the bus, unseen by me, a Volkswagen was driving toward me at full speed. I heard something, I saw something out of my left eye, the car hit me on the left side, my head smashed its windshield, I flew into the air and landed on the pavement on my right side, leaving me with, among other things, an unresolved hematoma in my right hip. For a while, I would occasionally collapse for no apparent reason. By the time I speak of now, I merely had pain from time to time. The pain I had to report was pain in my right hip.

  He asked me to sit in a chair and put out my legs. He held his hands under my feet. He was doing something called, colloquially, "growing arms and legs." (This is a technique much used by Charles and Frances Hunter.) That is not what it really is; it is more like a chiropractic adjustment by means of the Holy Spirit, usually. But I did not know any of that at this time. Not long before this, someone in the church had spoken of a time when they had received prayer for back pain. They reported that they had felt great warmth in the area affected when someone had prayed for them. Knowing nothing and wanting to learn, I paid attention to this story, and I said to myself, "So that's how God does it," thinking "that's how God *always* does it." So now I closed my eyes, trying hard to feel heat in my right hip. Then my guest preacher says, "There did you see it?" And I said, "Huh?" And he said, "Your foot, it grew." And I said, "Huh?" I was thinking that you can pivot the foot on the ankle pretty well, and I was not at all sure of anything. Then he asked me to stand and to tell him how it felt. Well, by golly, it felt just fine, thank you very much. And it did. The pain was gone. It has been pretty well gone ever since and that is over twenty years ago. [I believe that twenty years of relief compares fairly well to the results of the average doctor's visit.] That told me that healing could happen, because it happened to me.

Not too long thereafter I was visiting a parishioner in her eighties in her cabin in the mountains. Highland was hot, and she had a cabin up at Running Springs to spend the summer. We chatted. One of her concerns was that she could not clean her cabin as well as she would like to since her back was hurting her. As I was about to leave, I asked her if she wanted me to pray with her about anything. She wanted prayer for her back. Well, pastors pray for their people, so what could I do but pray? I prayed for her back to be healed. Then I got up to go. She walked me to the door. After I got a few steps from the door, she called to me, "Jim, Jim, the pain – it's gone." Outwardly, I said something very bland, like, "That's nice," but inwardly, I said, "Hooray" or "Hallelujah!" Before I knew that healing could happen; now I knew that God could make it happen through me. There were several other instances of God using me in healing prayer while I still lived in Highland. Then, in 1991, I was sent to my current church, the North Clairemont United Methodist Church, in San Diego.

Now I am going to speak of something some of you will find strange. It is sufficiently strange to the contemporary, secular mind-set that I am reluctant to speak of it for fear that I might alienate those whom I would have read further. But it is true. It is all true. I hope that truth will prove some sort of defense even for the mind of a committed materialist. It is also quite interesting. And it strongly tends to confirm the reality of the spiritual world. It is not something I intend to speak much of in this work, but it is interesting, it is true, and I did encounter it before I put together the elements of the pattern for healing a wounded spirit which I shall impart in this book, and, thus, if I am to recount how I got to where I wish now to take you, I suppose that we must go through this. Bear with me now.

It happened not long after I began to work at North Clairemont in San Diego. There had long been a Tuesday morning women's Bible study. It met in the Sanctuary. One time I had left something that I needed in the pulpit in the Sanctuary, and I recalled that I had done so on Tuesday morning. I waited for the study to end, and sometime thereafter, I went to get whatever it was I had left. There was one woman still there in the Sanctuary. I knew her well, and she was very fond of me. And now I am going to use false names. I nodded to her and said, "Hello, Eloise." And she said, in a deep and strange voice, "My name is not Eloise. My name is Hildegard." And she got up and began to come at me, looking for all the world as if she were going to attack me. I refused to believe that she would attack me and just stood there, arms at my side, awaiting her attack, and at the last moment, her facial expression changed, she put her arms around me and hugged me, and then she asked, "What happened?" I said, "I think I know," and I went to get a woman on staff, who I thought knew more about this than I did, to join us. This other person came, and she was there, but she mostly gave prayer support. I dealt with what manifested itself on that occasion. On four separate occasions, over the period of one and a half or two hours, two different entities, other than the woman herself, reported their presence, gave their names, and revealed something of themselves. This was the first encounter I was aware of with unclean spirits. I do not even recall if I got them to go on that occasion, although I think at least one did, perhaps both.

Over the course of the next few months, and of course the years since, I had encounters with hundreds of entities claiming to be other spirits speaking through persons before me whom they said they were not. I do not intend to speak much of this phenomenon here because the matter requires more space than I can give it here. However, I must say that evidence is massive that "demonization" is real. (The commonly used term "demonic possession" is inaccurate and a mistranslation of the Greek.) Every problem is *not* caused by demons, but demonization is far more widespread than most people realize.

Furthermore, there does also exist the phenomenon of Disassociative Identity Disorder (DID), formerly called Multiple Personality Disorder (MPD). (There are fashions in psychology, you know. Psychology is often more an art than a science. And recently the art is not so much Reubens, Matisse or Chagall, as it is Maplethorpe.) I mention this so that the reader may not suppose that I have confused the one with the other. A person may have both demonization and DID. The appropriate response to each is quite different. In my experience, demonization is far more common than DID. And, to repeat an important point, everything is *not* demons, and certainly not DID for that matter.

Let me also note that when I was next asked to deal with a person who wanted to be "delivered" of an unclean spirit, I spoke to her first about diet, exercise, medicines, rest, and every other natural phenomenon I could think of. However, she insisted that she had a demon. I did pray in Jesus name for the unclean spirit to leave her. After an interesting process, about which I will speak a little later, it did leave. There was physical evidence of something happening as I prayed, she reported a night and day change in how she felt after we prayed, and the family with whom she lived reported a night and day change in how she acted after this session. However, my point here is that I was not quick to assume demonization.

I am not afraid of demons. The name of Jesus Christ is far more powerful. (To speak of "the name of Jesus" does not mean merely to speak a name; it refers to the authority you have and know you have in your relationship with Jesus Christ.) Nor am I afraid to speak about unclean spirits, but it would require space beyond that available in this setting, and that is simply not my current focus. At this point, I know a fair amount about them. I have often found out how they came to a person, when they first came to a person, what event precipitated their entry, and what that person could do to keep himself or herself free of them. And, of course, hundreds of times, demons have been obliged to leave. Now let me repeat once more that not everything involves demons.

However, I did encounter demons in people before I began to sort out the principles which will constitute the body of this work, and it was, partially, in dealing with such issues that I discovered or assembled these principles. My role was simply that of pastor. If people had problems, and they wanted to come and talk, we would talk. And then I would deal with whatever we found as best I could. The results were often very helpful to people, and over time, I found the pattern I shall offer in this book to be generally helpful for a variety of situations.

Early on, I developed the habit of praying for God to be there, to protect and to guide. Early on, I developed the habit of asking the Holy Spirit to speak to the person coming for help to tell him, or her, what it was that we needed to deal with. God does give me "words of knowledge," something like what the naturalist might call an insight, but I prefer to work largely on the basis of what comes to the mind of the person seeking help. I try very hard to *not* plant ideas, and there are ways in which one can greatly improve the odds of avoiding that. So, first I asked God to show up and lead. Then I asked God to speak to the person seeking help. Then I asked that person to report what comes to them. That gave us our starting point.

I found that there often came to mind some very specific incident. Incidences of childhood molestation, physical trauma, abandonment, and severe illness were often early sources of later difficulty. These are the kinds of things which cause a person to *mis*-read themselves, others, men, women, God and life. These are the kinds of things that *may* also lead to demonic entry. These are the kinds of things that will often need to be dealt with in the "healing of memories," or "inner healing," or healing the wounds of the spirit.

One of the first things I supposed that we should do in response to these events was to forgive the perpetrators. Forgiveness is much spoken of in Christian circles. Jesus says some very clear and strong things about our need to forgive. I had already heard it alleged that arthritis was related to unforgiveness. (I have had no experiential confirmation of this correlation, but it still sounds plausible to me.) So I was sure that we needed to walk people through forgiveness. One emphasis I had that differed from some others was that the person needed to be honest. I did not believe that fake forgiveness was all that helpful, nor that God was too deeply offended by honesty. I also began to realize that forgiveness did *not* mean it was not wrong, nor that it did not hurt, nor that it should be forgotten, nor that it necessarily included a restoration of trust. We will have a section on this later.

Early on I discovered another Christian principle which I find to be abandoned, no, rejected by many in the Christian world: Mourning. Jesus said "blessed are those who mourn, for they shall be comforted." Frankly, it looks very much like what the secular world calls "the grief process." It is not a place to stay, but it is often a place to go through, and people have often felt a need to try to jump over it. Jumping over does not work. The denial of feeling which some Christians seem to propose is not

Christianity, it is stoicism. Mourning will be dealt with in detail too.

Another Christian word much used is "repentance." I supposed, and quite rightly, that we need to "repent," or turn away from wrong actions. We need to acknowledge the rightness of God's word, the error of our conduct not in conformity to it, and commit to try to do the right thing hereafter, especially any misconduct seemingly related to or arising from the original spiritual trauma. This needs its own section also.

Then I saw that in response to the traumatic events that misshape us, we acquire wrong ideas, wrong beliefs. We need to "repent" of those too. However, you cannot just pull weeds and expect them to stay gone; you've got to plant some attractive flowers to take over the plot of ground. So it was not just repenting, but there was also to be a transformation of the mind. God can do that too, and it is also a biblical principle, and will have its own section.

Of course we ask Jesus to heal. I may know less about how this works than any other element! But it does.

This element may be a part of the prior one, or it may not. At some point, I came to ask people, after we had done all of the above, to look at the specific scene once again. I asked them for some description so that I would know that they had a very specific vision in mind. Then I would ask them to tell me if they saw anything in the spiritual realm. I did *not* ask them to *envision* it or to *imagine* it; I asked them to tell me *if* they saw anything. Most of the time, they did. Eventually, if they saw anything at all, they invariably saw some sign of the presence and care of God. (They may also have seen signs of something unholy there, but God invariably manifested far greater power.)

At this point, I have sketched, in very rough outline, much of what I will offer in the pages that follow. There is more about how to do it, and about why it is biblically and psychologically sound. There is more to illustrate how it works, and what its benefits can be. I will begin with a few illustrative examples that the reader might sense some of the potential benefit of what I speak. Then I will give some general understanding of how both hurt and healing happen, and then a more detailed rendering of the means by which you and God may heal the wounds of the spirit, and with that healing, find a release from many afflictions - physical, spiritual, emotional, social and more.

Chapter One: Introductory Examples of Healing by Spiritual Means

Shingles Healed in a Moment

A woman came to my office. She had had a variety of recurring problems, and now she wanted help. She did not know the reasons for her various afflictions. Additionally, at this time, she also had shingles, and it was especially affecting her left eye. Leaving out a number of steps for the moment, I asked God to bring to mind what we needed to work on that day. She began to get an image of herself as a little girl. As the image unfolded, eventually it became clear that it was a memory, she saw herself being molested by a family member who ought to have been a person of the greatest trust, as she sat on the edge of her bed, her face, especially her left eye, being shoved against a bedpost. Armed with this knowledge, we prayed again. She felt better immediately, and the shingles did not run their course. It left. I do not now recall if it was instantly or if it was by the next morning, but it did not run its course; it left. An experience with spiritual consequences read out decades later in a physical ailment. When requested, God revealed the spiritual origin, and, when known, the physical ailment was healed by prayer, using the kinds of biblical principles I will unfold in this book.

A Thirty Year Cycle of Pain Ended

Across several years, a woman came to my office for prayer for pain. She did not say more about the pain, and I did not ask. I prayed with her, and the pain diminished or left. Yet this pain returned again and again across the years. One time she came to me in tears. It was the same ailment, but the pain was much greater now. Before the problem might have caused pain or, occasionally, laid her up for a couple of days in a month, but now the pain was lasting for a couple of weeks, and it was much more severe. She had been to see doctors, and they told her that the only remedy was to get a hysterectomy. She felt she was too young for this, and asked for prayer again. This was the first time I came to know that her pain was related to her monthly period.

We chatted quietly for a while. I asked her when the pain began. She said that she had "always had it."

INTRODUCTORY EXAMPLES OF HEALING BY SPIRITUAL MEANS

We chatted quietly a bit more, and then I asked her the same question in another way. "How old was she when the she first felt this pain?" I asked. "Oh, about twelve," she answered. "Well," I went on at some point, "knowing that the pain is related to your monthly period brings to mind the possibility that it is related to some trauma in the area of your sexuality. Were you ever molested?" "No," was the immediate response, and then, "Well, ... not really." "Oh?" I said, "What happened?" "Well, I was at someone else's house, and this man tried to do something, but I locked myself in the bathroom and told him to go away. He left, and I ran home and told my mother." She said. "How old were you when this happened?" I asked. She answered, "Twelve."

Now, armed with this knowledge, *and using the pattern I will discuss in this book*, we prayed again. The result was this: A thirty year cycle of recurring pain, now so severe that she was nearly incapacitated for half of each month and so severe that major surgery was recommended by more than one doctor, was ended. It is now some years since that day. The pain has not come back, and she never had the surgery. An experience which was traumatizing to her spirit when she was twelve had consequences in her life for roughly thirty years thereafter. The consequence was recurring and increasing pain. When the spiritual wound was healed, the physical manifestation fell away.

Colon Healed, Surgery Cancelled

More recently, a man came to my office for prayer. He already had surgery scheduled. He did not come for prayer for healing. He came for prayer of commiseration. This was a serious surgery he had scheduled and one with lasting and unpleasant consequences, and so he wanted God's strength to get him through this ordeal and the life-long ordeal after the surgery. The surgery scheduled was to remove his colon. There had been a history of colon problems in his family. He had had colon problems for many years. For some years, the doctors had told him it was only a matter of time before he would have to have his colon removed in order to be sure that he did not get cancer and die from that. Now, they felt, was the time, and so did he. He was resigned to the surgery, but he wanted prayer to get through the ordeal of the surgery

INTRODUCTORY EXAMPLES OF HEALING BY SPIRITUAL MEANS

and the necessity of the alternate system of waste removal after it.

I told him that I would, of course, pray for God's strength for him, but I said these things sometimes have spiritual causes. Would he like us to pray and see if God might have some healing for him? "Well," he assured me, "ten years before," he had done significant work with a pastor/counselor who had previously been in the area, and he felt that he had dealt with everything he knew. I knew the pastor of whom he spoke, and I said that indeed he was a good and able man, but still there might be something else. Would he like to see if there was anything else to discover? He was willing.

I asked God to bring to mind anything that we might need to work on which was related to this physical ailment. Eventually, a memory came to mind of this man, as a boy, fishing with his father. He, the boy, had caught a fish, and he wanted his father's attention and approval, but he did not get it. The father was caught up in his own fishing concerns and had no time for his son. The son felt rejected – again. While this event was doubtless important in itself, it also stood for a generalized experience of rejection by his father.

Again, we, meaning mostly he, had a little talk with God. He went through the steps I will outline in this book. There were tears. There was release, and he said he felt better. He left. I did not see him to talk to for about two weeks. I asked him then how he was. He said that he had quit taking medicines he had been taking for years, and that for the first time in years, he had been "symptom free." I did not know what that meant, not knowing what his symptoms had been, but it sounded good to me. And he reported that he had also canceled the surgery. Periodically after that, I would ask him how he was, and he was always fine. About six months after the scheduled surgery had been canceled, he had another colonoscopy. The doctor reported that his colon was now fine. There were no pre-cancerous polyps, as there had been before, there was one benign non-pre-cancerous polyp, his colon was clean, and he should see the doctor again in about six months. His colon had physically changed, and the only intervention was prayer in Jesus' name, using the biblical principles I will discus in this book. An event did damage to his spirit decades before. It had deleterious physical consequences for him for years, leading to a planned removal of his colon. In the space of an hour or two, a problem in the spiritual realm was found and healed, and this lead to healing in the physical realm of serious ailments of many years standing to which major surgery had been thought to be the only solution.

Marriage Healed

Another man came to my office. He had committed adultery. I had met with both him and his wife before. He was very upset that he had done so hurtful a thing to his wife. He did not know why he would do it, although he knew full well that he had. He was inclined to think that "the answer" was simply to make a better resolve, to simply "force" himself to do what he thought he should do by an act of will. This is not an unworthy response, nor is it wrong, but it is often inadequate. After some season of conversation, I asked him if he was willing for us to pray a bit, and he was.

After some of the preliminary prayers I will note later, I asked God's Spirit to bring to his spirit something relevant to our present concern. Before long he began to get a memory of himself watching TV as a child. He was lying on the floor in front of the TV in the living room. Only he and his older brother were at home. His older brother was watching TV with him. After a while, his older brother came to him and began to molest him. Now the older brother was young too, but this was molestation. Before long, it became apparent that the man I was ministering to had done many things throughout his life to "prove" to himself that he was not a fit object of penetration, that he "was a man." We went through a number of prayers that shall be later noted. There were tears, and there was emotional release, and there seems subsequently to be a substantial change of conduct, a change in thought patterns and desires, and a greater enjoyment of life.

In significant part, this childhood event was an underlying cause of conduct years later that he did not want, much regretted, and has now successfully left behind. When we began, he had no conscious knowledge that this incident had ever even happened. If he had known of it, he probably would not have considered it the cause of any later conduct on his part. But he came to know of it, and it was dealt with in the way to be explained in this book, and it has led to change in areas not previously thought to be related.

Many Ailments Have Spiritual Origins, and Spiritual Cures

I could give you many further examples, of physical afflictions healed and of relational and social functioning problems healed, but I share these few examples to introduce you slightly to my subject. I do so at this early point to engage the reader's interest. I fear that the naturalism or materialism of our age may lead some to doubt the reality or utility of the matters of which I speak. What I intend to speak of here is real, and it can have massive beneficial consequences. I believe that the principles and procedures I shall unfold can be used successfully to obtain healing from a broad range of problems and conditions. I have used these introductory examples also because they are of substantial matters and with results, in some cases, subsequently confirmed by doctors, and thus examples I hope not easily dismissed by the reader as mere psychosomatic flukes or trifles. The principles I shall unfold are theologically sound, psychologically sound, of enormous practical benefit, and their effectiveness has been confirmed in practice many times over. I also believe that this book can be a means for a pastor or other counselor to learn the principles and procedures it contains with sufficient clarity to begin to use them successfully in counseling others.

I want to speak of healing. I want to speak of healing many ailments, including physical ailments, by spiritual means. This healing comes, in part, by calling upon God to help. This healing also comes, in part, by the application of spiritual principles which I find declared in scripture and confirmed in life. What I shall speak of is something I have seen work in practice many times. It has produced benefits, often spectacular benefits, many times. I believe that what I have discovered is a pattern that can be used for healing by others. This pattern can certainly be used by one who stands as a counselor to another to help them with a great variety of afflictions. It can also be used by individuals who have intractable problems of unknown origins as a way to begin to understand what is troubling them. It may also be used by individuals to work through their own problems, although I think it is generally better to have another work with you, and it will sometimes not be possible to work through matters without some trustworthy other.

The matters of which I speak affect physical health, but they do not affect *only* physical health. Persons I have seen have also previously seen psychiatrists, psychologists and various other counselors, reporting many difficulties. The afflictions they present may detrimentally impact their ability to interact with people, their ability to hold a job, their ability to manage their finances, their ability to keep their living spaces in reasonable order, their ability to achieve desired goals or even to *have* much in the way of goals, their ability to trust God or people, and their ability to have hope and enjoy life.

I see this book with more than one potential audience. Surely I intend it for the pastor and lay prayer counselor who is open to moving in the gifts of the Spirit and would like to increase his or her knowledge and ability in this area. (Some persons whom I have prayed for began immediately to use similar prayers to help others, and with, they report, much benefit.) I would hope that some persons in the fields of psychology and medicine would wish also to explore the insights and principles I offer here – after all, based upon the few examples I have already given, my work does "invade" "their domain." I also hope to have some general readers, persons with individual hurts they cannot explain and persons with deep concerns for friends or family members who have recurring problems they cannot explain, who might be led to recognize in new ways the reality and power of God for healing. I hope also to have some Christian readers who do not believe that God can *or should* work in the ways I will expound, people who tend to believe that emotions are not to be dealt with but rather "stuffed," and that the command to "just" do what you should is always sufficient to achieve any proper Christian goal, and that anything further is an accommodation to evil. I disagree, and I will speak of this later.

INTRODUCTORY EXAMPLES OF HEALING BY SPIRITUAL MEANS

There are many kinds of divine healing. There are a variety of ways of praying for physical healing. Some simply command healing. Some do things which are often much like a chiropractic adjustment by means of the Holy Spirit. There are those who are led to work almost exclusively from "words of knowledge."

(One time I was leading an introductory workshop on prayer for healing and I wanted to illustrate what a "word of knowledge" was to the participants. After telling them that this was a gift I did not have, I illustrated it by saying, "for example if Joe had a problem with his right knee, and Sue had a problem with her left foot." Later, in the practicum time, we discovered that Joe did have a problem with his right knee and Sue did have a problem with her left foot! That told me that God did speak to me that way, but I just was not accustomed to listen. That may well be the case for you also. A "word of knowledge" is a word or image or sympathetic pain that indicates a problem in another. The fact that God reveals something which the one proclaiming could not know is itself an indication that God intends to heal the problem indicated, and the hearing of a problem by one who has the problem from one who could not know about it in any natural way is a powerful encouragement to seek and accept help. With the occasional rare exception, I do *not use* "words of knowledge" in the ministry pattern I now write about.)

There is deliverance ministry, wherein unclean spirits which have, in some manner, invaded an individual or, sometimes, a place, are cast out. This is a perfectly valid and enormously helpful ministry, but it also is one with which I deal only in passing in this discussion of inner healing.

There is also, of course, what is called medicine, and I do not deny, dismiss, denigrate or diminish the usefulness of medical treatment. All of these kinds of healing can happen and are useful, but they are not my focus here. I am focusing on one particular kind of healing process.

The subject which I undertake has been called "healing the wounded spirit," "healing of memories," and "inner healing." Its undergirding premise is that there can be things which we humans experience that cause us spiritual harm, or wound us in our spirits, and that these things can subsequently have damaging consequences in

INTRODUCTORY EXAMPLES OF HEALING BY SPIRITUAL MEANS

our physical health, emotional health, ability to develop healthy relationships, work habits, expectation of success or defeat, and so on. It is further supposed that dealing only with the visible symptoms of such damage is often much like cutting off the tops of weeds: The garden may look better for a season, but the weeds grow back. You need to uproot the weeds, and then to plant some appropriate flowers if you want a healthy garden.

In the next chapter, I will offer a defense of the main premise underlying this approach: Spiritually damaging things, sometime long past and forgotten, can have consequences in many areas of life years later. Then I will address the damaging consequences and theological unsoundness of denial. In a later chapter, I will explain how I have most commonly employed the principles that follow so that the reader can better see how to use the spiritual principles that are discussed thereafter. I intend this volume to be practically useful as well as theologically, spiritually and psychologically sound.

JIM HILL

Chapter Two: The Law of Cause and Effect Has Not Been Repealed, or Effects Have Causes and It's Okay to Look for Them

A man reaps what he sows. – Galatians 6:7
An undeserved curse does not come to rest.
– Proverbs 26:2

For a time when I was in Highland, I dated a Catholic charismatic lady. One time I went to her house for dinner. She still had some cooking preparations to do. In the meantime, she handed me a book to look at. She had been taking a course in alcoholism counseling. The book she handed me was *Another Chance: Hope and Help for the Alcoholic Family* by Sharon Wegscheider. My friend pointed to a page and a half summary of one of the rolls people take on in an alcoholic family and told me to read it. After I read a little bit, I began to laugh out loud. I didn't like it, but it fit; it was me.

That was the first time I knew that some things about me did not "just happen." It was not "just the way it was." It was not "just the way men are." It was not "just the way I was." It was not "just the way life is." It was not "just the way 'it' is." It was not inevitable. There had been a way in, and that meant to me that there was a way out. I did not know what that was. I might never know very clearly either the way in or the way out, but just knowing that things were caused and not inevitable was freeing in itself.

My father had a drinking problem, and that had consequences for the family, including me. Over time, I read several books about adult children of alcoholics, and I learned a good deal about the dynamics of an alcoholic family. I find that the dynamics of the alcoholic family apply to a host of dysfunctional family settings. Others in the family system adjust to make a dysfunctional system work as nearly normal as seems possible. We keep secrets. We make excuses. And then we have our own individual adjustments. One becomes the hero, who works hard, taking responsibility to make everything work out for all. Another becomes a bad boy, getting attention through doing bad. Another becomes a mascot, cute, given attention for being cute, and ineffectual, and so on. There is much more to this subject, and for any who sense some special recognition here, I advise you to read two or three books in the field to see if there is more for you to pursue here. My point in this context is merely to point out that it was at this point that I learned something about the spiritual causation of attitudes, expectations, fears, social relations, and thought life. My concern in this chapter is to establish that effects have causes.

Effects Have Causes

It should be axiomatic. It should be accepted. And by some it is. But by many it is not. Effects have causes. It is something like the scientific axiom that every action has an equal and opposite reaction. It is a basic scientific assumption, is it not? How can one determine cause and effect without the assumption that effects have causes? We work with the assumption that if something is, it has arisen from somewhere. But does not science everywhere work with that assumption? Yes, it does. Should not faith borrow such wisdom from science? No. It has no need to. Christian faith has long since had this wisdom. It was Christian faith that has given it to science.

Paul says in Galatians 6:7: "A man reaps what he sows." Here we have the law of sowing and reaping. Reasoning backwards then, if one reaps bitterness, then one must have sown bitterness somehow. Does it not follow? Perhaps an enemy got into your field to sow that bitterness, but that bitterness got there somehow. Did it not?

In Deuteronomy 28, there is a long list of blessings and curses. In verses 1 through 15, Moses tells the people that if they do things as God has advised, they will experience many blessings. They will prosper in their flocks and fields, in the businesses, in their health and in their families. Then, in verses 16 through 68, he tells them that if they do not do things as God has told them to, they will have misery. Their health will be damaged, their fields and flocks will suffer, they will be subject to attack and conquest by other nations, and their lives will generally be miserable. From a Christian point of view, this passage must surely suggest that detrimental consequences might have been caused by wrong actions on the part of the believer. From any point of view, it is clear that Moses believes that God has passed on some

THE LAW OF CAUSE AND EFFECT HAS NOT BEEN REPEALED, OR EFFECTS HAVE CAUSES AND IT'S OKAY TO LOOK FOR THEM

rules for living the following of which will have many beneficial consequences and the disobedience to which will have many deleterious consequences. Non-Christians, even if they were not in agreement with Moses on every particular, must sense some truth that conduct can affect consequences. Biblically based Christians should have even broader and more specific agreement with Moses.

Proverbs 26:2 says: "Like a fluttering sparrow or a darting swallow, an undeserved curse does not land." If you accept the Bible as authoritative, as we Christians do, then that is strong evidence that when a curse (or a misfortune in general?) has been received, then there is likely to have been some reason. The Hebrew word for "curse," *qelalah* and from *qalal*, means "to make small," or "to diminish," therefore the notion that "curse" may mean misfortune in general should not offend. [Let the reader recall that I see myself arguing with the boot-strap Christian at one moment (You do everything by pulling on your own boot-straps.), and the anti-supernaturalist non-Christian the next.]

In the Lord's Prayer, there is a strong implication

that our ability to receive forgiveness is contingent upon our having given it. "Forgive us our debts, *as we also have forgiven our debtors.*" [Emphasis added.] – Matthew 6:12. After giving the Lord's Prayer to his disciples, Jesus goes on to make an even stronger statement as Matthew records it in 6:14-15: "For if you forgive men when they sin against you, your heavenly Father will also forgive you. But if you do not forgive men their sins, your Father will not forgive your sins." My point here is not the necessity of forgiveness, we shall discuss that later, but the probability that our actions may have consequences, even our actions of the soul, and here that is explicitly stated by Jesus.

A Bitter Root

In Deuteronomy 29:18, Moses makes another interesting statement, with an interesting interpretive history. There it says: "Make sure there is no man or woman, clan or tribe among you today whose heart turns away from the Lord our God to go and worship the gods of those nations; make sure there is no root among you that produces such bitter poison." Here he seems to be saying

THE LAW OF CAUSE AND EFFECT HAS NOT BEEN REPEALED, OR EFFECTS HAVE CAUSES AND IT'S OKAY TO LOOK FOR THEM

that apostasy, or worship of other gods, will prove to be a root that eventually produces a bitter fruit. A more general point might be that such apostasy, or consequential action, may not produce misfortune immediately, but it will prove, over time, to be a root of much bitterness, or misfortune, later.

The author of Hebrews makes much the same point, calling upon this same metaphor of Moses. In 12:15, he says: "See to it that no one misses the grace of God and that no bitter root grows up to cause trouble and defile many." This verse too, as in Deuteronomy, is set in a context emphasizing holy living. Obviously, the specific application is that if one lives in a godly manner, one will not experience such bitter fruit as one will if one does not live in a godly manner, but my point here is that present bitterness may have prior roots.

In recent years, a "doctrine of bitter root" has arisen. When one does not interpret but extrapolate, there is always risk of excess or error, and I suspect that some of what has been done in this area may have been excessive; fortunately I am too little acquainted with such work to know of any errors. My point here is to suggest that these passages also support the notion that actions have consequences. Furthermore, it adds a new element: These passages also suggest that the consequences, while bitter, may be delayed. The cause will be as a root, not apparent above ground, but no less the cause of the bitterness experienced. In short, here is biblical warrant for the idea that current problems may have distant and not immediately known causes.

Generational Sin

Exodus 20:5 adds another corollary to this law of cause and effect. It says: "You shall not bow down to them or worship them [other gods or idols]; for I the Lord your God am a jealous God, punishing the children for the sin of the fathers to third and fourth generation of those who hate me, but showing love to a thousand generations of those who love and keep my commandments." This indicates that our misdeeds can have consequences for succeeding generations. But that should be no surprise. Have you not heard of innumerable studies indicating that the child of an alcoholic is more likely to have certain problems, or that an abuser was almost surely himself

THE LAW OF CAUSE AND EFFECT HAS NOT BEEN REPEALED, OR EFFECTS HAVE CAUSES AND IT'S OKAY TO LOOK FOR THEM

abused, or that most men in prison grew up in homes without fathers, and so on? Thus, the reality of the consequences of sin in one generation upon the next is confirmed. By the way, this verse also points out that fidelity to God also has trans-generational benefits. This too should be easy to understand. The gracious home is more likely to raise healthy children, and so on. But our general focus in this work is on dealing with problems and so we shall look more closely at the unpleasant part of this statement. By the way, this phenomenon is often called "generational sin."

Let me say here, that I do not think that God out of spite chooses to curse the innocent children of malevolent parents, and I am supported in this by Ezekiel 18:14-17, and many other passages. But we have here an expression of how it seemed to those who saw this phenomenon at work. God has so constructed man and life that it works *as if* that were so. There are also some spiritual things that can happen across generations, but that may be more detail than we need now. Once again, my general point here is that actions have consequences, and that the current consequences may be caused by actions not immediately apparent.

The Spirit Affects the Body

There are a number of passages in Proverbs which suggest a correlation between specific spiritual conditions and physical ailments or health. I note some of them below. Pastor Henry Wright has done much to find correlation between specific physical ailments and specific spiritual causes, as noted in his book *A More Excellent Way* (Pleasant Valley Church, Thomaston, GA, 2001). I cannot affirm all his claims, but I note that he affirms the principle of cause and effect which I affirm more generally, and I credit him with having called to my attention the verses from Proverbs noted below:

Proverbs 13:12: "Hope deferred makes the heart sick."

Proverbs 14:30: "A heart at peace gives life to the body, but envy rots the bones."

Proverbs 15:13: "A happy heart makes the face cheerful, but heartache crushes the spirit."

THE LAW OF CAUSE AND EFFECT HAS NOT BEEN REPEALED, OR EFFECTS HAVE CAUSES AND IT'S OKAY TO LOOK FOR THEM

Proverbs 15:30: "A cheerful look brings joy to the heart, And good news gives health to the bones."

Proverbs 16:24: "Pleasant words are a honeycomb, sweet to the soul and healing to the bones."

There are many other biblical passages which indicate in a more general way that there are consequences, good or bad, to following or not following the ways of God. I note a few of those below:

Exodus 15:26 says that if you do what is right God will protect you and not bring upon his followers the diseases He brought upon the Egyptians.

Leviticus 26:14-17 says that if we do not do what we are told to do, we will experience "sudden terror, wasting disease and fever that will destroy your sight and drain away your life" and many other unpleasant things.

I Samuel 15:22 says that "to obey is better than sacrifice" and notes consequences for disobedience.

Daniel 9:11 attributes the misfortunes of Israel in Babylon to their disobedience.

Malachi 2:1-2, tells the priests that they had better honor God or they will experience curses.

In Matthew 7:24, Jesus says that those who hear and do what He says will have a firm foundation, and those who do not, will not.

In Luke 11:28, Jesus says again that "blessed rather are those who hear the word of God and obey it."

James, in 1:25, says, "But the man who looks intently into the perfect law that gives freedom, and continues to do this, not forgetting what he has heard, but doing it – he will be blessed in what he does."

All these verses I cite to establish two things in our understanding. One is that actions have consequences, effects have causes, or consequences have causes. The other is that the causes may be spiritual. Spiritual causes can have physical and social and financial and many other consequences.

Medical Research Confirms the Biblical Principle

There is also a substantial body of research which confirms the correlation I find between physical ailments and spiritual causes and cures. Some of such studies were noted and summarized by Dean Ornish in his book *Love and Survival* (HarperCollins, New York, 1999).

THE LAW OF CAUSE AND EFFECT HAS NOT BEEN REPEALED, OR EFFECTS HAVE CAUSES AND IT'S OKAY TO LOOK FOR THEM

While his focus was upon the benefits of warm social relations, I think the data reported also reveals the correlation between the wounded spirit and physical ailments, which is one part of my argument. I note some of his conclusions and a number of the studies he cites below:

"Love and intimacy are among the most powerful factors in health and illness.... I am not aware of any other factor in medicine – not diet, not smoking, not exercise, not stress, not genetics, not drugs, not surgery – that has a greater impact on our quality of life, incidence of illness, and premature death from all causes." (pp. 2-3)

"Loneliness and isolation ... increase the likelihood of disease and premature death from all causes by 200 to 500 percent or more." (p. 13)

Victor Frankl, a physician and psychiatrist who was imprisoned in Auschwitz during WW II, found that concentration camp inmate "survival was much less a factor of age or infirmity that their ability to find a sense of meaning." (p. 16)

A Yale study of 199 men and 40 women undergoing angiography found that "those who felt the most loved and supported had substantially less blockage in the arteries of their hearts." (pp. 24-25)

A Case Western Reserve University study of 10,000 married men with no prior history of angina found that those with risk factors such as high cholesterol, high blood pressure, age, diabetes and electrocardiogram abnormalities were over twenty times more likely to develop new angina in the next five years, but "those who answered 'yes' to the simple question, 'Does your wife show you her love?' had significantly less angina even when they had high levels of these risk factors." (p. 25)

A study of 8,500 men with no history of duodenal ulcers were studied over five years. Eventually, 254 of these men developed ulcers. "Those who had reported a low level of perceived love and support from their wives when they entered the study had over *twice as many* ulcers as the other men. Those who answered, 'My wife does not love me' had *three times* as many ulcers." (p. 26)

In the 1950's, 126 healthy Harvard men were randomly chosen and asked about their sense of closeness to their mothers and fathers. Their medical records were reviewed 35 years later. Ninety-one percent of those who

THE LAW OF CAUSE AND EFFECT HAS NOT BEEN REPEALED, OR EFFECTS HAVE CAUSES AND IT'S OKAY TO LOOK FOR THEM

did not perceive themselves to have warm relationships with their mothers had serious diseases in midlife, while only 45% of those who felt they had had warm relationships had such diseases. Eighty-two percent of those who felt little warmth with their father had serious midlife disease, while only 50% of those who had a high degree of warmth had such disease. (p. 33)

In another study, "95% of subjects who rated their parents low in parental caring had serious diseases diagnosed in midlife, and only 29% of those who rated their parents high in caring had such diagnoses." (p. 35)

In a Carnegie-Mellon University study, 276 healthy volunteers were infected with the rhinovirus that causes the common cold. Those with a poor social network had *four times* the risk of developing a cold than those with a good social network. Social support greatly increased resistance to disease even when infected. (p. 62)

Personally, time and again, I see that the death of a loved one leads to illness for a surviving spouse, and, sometimes, to death shortly thereafter. Things that affect our spirits affect us in many ways. A number of times across the years, I have noticed that I can have worked long hours, be tired, be exposed to germs, and *not* get sick; then when I have worked long hours, am tired, have been exposed to germs, *and* experience stress, I get sick. Emotional stress is a significant factor in physical sickness. And all of this is presented to bolster the argument that effects have causes.

An Aside: Science Is a Child of Christian Faith

Let me make a small aside. Previously I noted that I supposed that the law of cause and effect was well established in science. I furthermore suppose that many think that science and Christian faith are in some kind of conflict. This I deny. Science is a child of Christian faith. I invite the reader to read *Science and the Modern Mind* by Alfred North Whitehead, no Christian he. He attributes the rise of science to two assumptions of, to use his term, the Judeo-Christian world view: 1) That this world matters, and 2) That to study it is a holy work, revelatory of the mind of God. He further argues that societies with world-views, or religions, without these ideas may have produced great inventions, but they never produced the scientific method. Dear reader, as some

THE LAW OF CAUSE AND EFFECT HAS NOT BEEN REPEALED, OR EFFECTS HAVE CAUSES AND IT'S OKAY TO LOOK FOR THEM

check on this theory, I ask you to ask yourself in what lands did the scientific method arise? And in what religion were those lands steeped? I also think that the belief in meliorability or perfectibility was important. For that consider II Corinthians 3:18 and J. B. Bury's *The Idea of Progress*. Max Weber has a number of studies reflecting upon the social consequences of religious values which it would also be fruitful to peruse. Science is a child of Christian faith. Scientism is not, but then it is not science.

In Summary

To summarize again, all the preceding discussion was presented to establish two things: Actions have consequences, consequences have causes, or effects have causes, And the causes may be spiritual. Spiritual causes can have physical and social and financial and many other consequences. Granting that that may be so, then what might we do to minister healing to persons with problems which might have spiritual causes? How do we discern the causes? How do we make a difference? Those are the concerns of subsequent chapters. In the next chapter, I will speak of the inadequacy of denial as a therapeutic technique, or, of the necessity and virtue of facing facts. I will also note that the finding of *disorder* presupposes the reality of some sort of *order*, and how that conflicts with some contemporary assumptions. Then I will give an overview of how I have most commonly employed the principles that follow. The chapters after that will each develop particular principles which, when applied, can sometimes help enormously. These principles are each sound both biblically and psychologically. Then I will speak of another way in which one can, usually, have assurance of God's presence, protection and love, both in the past and, as a consequence, in the future also.

Chapter Three:
If You Live in the State of Denial, Move

They dress the wound of my people as though it were not serious.
"Peace, peace," they say, when there is no peace.
- Jeremiah 6:14

If you do not have a problem, great! Then you have nothing to face. But if you do have a problem, then you should try to figure it out! In my experience, questions we ask are more likely to be answered than questions we do not ask. In my experience, refusing to deal with a situation does not improve the odds of it getting better. If you wish to play the ostrich and stick your head in the sand, the only likely result is that you leave your backside vulnerable.

We all have reluctance, often unconscious, to deal with problems to which we do not think there are answers. If we cannot conceive of a solution, then to try to solve the "insoluble" will merely lead to frustration, which we earnestly wish to avoid. Furthermore, if this problem leads us to do things we think (or we think others think) are bad *and* we think it is insoluble, then we are doubly determined to not see it since to see it would mean to find fault *not* with some *aspect* of our lives, but with *the very core of our being.* One rejoinder I have to that fear is this: The God I know can deal with far, far more than is generally thought.

Evangelical Christians also, often, have an additional problem to overcome in dealing with reality. Many have imbibed a theology that believes *all* problems are merely the result of a defective conscious will. If you *just* do the right thing, it will all be right. This may be so, but what if you find you cannot quite get yourself to do the right thing? If you *just* think the right thing, it will be okay. This may be so, but what if you cannot quite get yourself to think the right thing? If you *just* pray, it will be fine. This can be so, but what if you pray, and you still have thoughts, attitudes, feelings or conduct which are not right? Some give up on the difficult quest to think, feel and do right, and change their understanding of right and wrong to correspond to their stubborn feelings. Others try to "stuff" their feelings and act right despite a great inner struggle. That is right enough and perhaps even noble, but it is not much fun. I believe that God can give us better. Others try to "stuff" their feelings and do the right thing and fail and feel horribly condemned. Despite the possible pain and frustration involved, I recommend that we try to deal with reality.

Then too, some labor under the belief that Christians should not have problems and therefore should not be troubled about things, and therefore acknowledging any trouble is to believe themselves unsaved sinners. Since Jesus has overcome the world, we should have too, they might believe, but that is nonsense. Jesus said, "In this world you will have trouble. But take heart! I have overcome the world." [John 16:33] Because He *has* overcome the world, we *will* be able to. It is already achieved *for* us; it is not already achieved *in* us. However, by virtue of what God has made possible, it *can* be achieved *in* us too.

Finally, some are hindered in dealing with emotional things because they think they should not have emotions! Emotions are great. They are what moves you. That's what "emotion" means. Some believe that

Christians, or perhaps anyone who "has it together," should not be troubled by things and thus should not have feelings about anything. But this is not Christianity; it is stoicism.

Many Christians will recall memorizing John 11:35, as a way to get a gold star for memorizing a verse without having to work too hard: "Jesus wept." In Luke 7:31-35, Jesus finds fault with a people who would neither dance nor cry. In Matthew 16:23, Jesus expresses anger with Peter, and in Matthew 17:17, He expresses anger with his disciples in general. Jesus had emotions. That should mean that it is okay for Christians to have emotions. God gave us emotions. Emotions are a part of the image of God in which we are made.

Now let me argue the case for dealing with reality from an even more demanding Christian perspective, but the non-Christian reader may follow to see how sound he finds these arguments. In the Sermon on the Mount, recorded in Matthew 5:21-48, Jesus declares that not only our actions matter, but also our very thoughts: "You have heard that it was said to the people long ago, 'Do not murder, and anyone who murders will be subject to judgment.' But I tell you that anyone who is angry with his brother will be subject to judgment." [Matthew 5:21-22a] This might suggest that recurring troubling thoughts, even if we do not act upon them, might be a sign of trouble with which it might be appropriate for us to deal.

In Matthew 12:36-37, we find that Jesus says that our words matter: "But I tell you that men will have to give account on the day of judgment for every careless word they have spoken. For by your words you will be acquitted, and by your words you will be condemned." This might suggest that recurring troubling words, even if no one else hears them, might be a sign of trouble with which we might wish to deal.

Then in Matthew 15:31-46, we find Jesus discussing the division of sheep and goats, the saved and the condemned, on the day of judgment, and some will enter into the joy of the Father and some will go to eternal punishment. Here we find that whatsoever we did to one of the least of his brothers, which includes sisters, or whatsoever we failed to do, may have eternal consequences. Taken together, these passages argue that our deeds, words and thoughts can all be matters of consequence, and thus if there is something amiss in any of those areas, we might want to try to sort it out.

Jesus adds an additional dimension in John 9:41. There Jesus is disputing with some Pharisees. He implies that there might be some excuse for those who could not be expected to know right from wrong, but for those who do know, *or who claim to know*, the responsibility is clear. His words are: "If you were blind, you would not be guilty of sin; but now that you claim you can see, your guilt remains."

Extrapolating from this passage, we might say that when one began a course of wrong conduct, in a response to wrong received, and especially if it was as a child or in some other kind of ignorance, that one might not then have full responsibility, but that once one "knows better," one does. Perhaps we can also say that you may not have caused your wrong feelings or conduct, but now that you know they are wrong, you have a responsibility to do something about it.

Here are some more disquieting verses. In Matthew 10:26-27, Mark 4:22, Luke 8:17, and Luke 12:2-

3, Jesus points out that there is nothing which is hidden which will not be revealed. This means several things. God knows what's going on. Hiding it from public notice or from your spouse or from the police or from the church does not mean it does not happen or is not real. Furthermore, this suggests that there will be consequences at some point in time. God's word *is* for eternity, but it is *not only* for the time to come; *it is also for now*, for eternity includes now. Therefore, I see here a suggestion that hidden problems may well also read out in our lives on earth, at least in time. This would suggest that it might be well to let God deal with it when a matter has become a mess or perhaps even before it has become a full-blown mess.

In Jeremiah 6:14, Jeremiah speaks of false prophets and false priests who "dress the wound of my people as though it were not serious. 'Peace, peace,' they say, when there is no peace." To proclaim peace when there is no peace is no virtue. To tell a man with a broken arm that his arm is not broken because you wish to help him avoid the pain of setting it is not virtue; it is folly at best, and more nearly, vice. It will set in a misshapen manner, with diminished use, and other damage possible.

Here is a cry by Jeremiah to not play Nefertiti, The Queen of "De-Nial." Talk to people in any addictive behaviors group, or any recovery group, and I am sure that they will tell you that one of the greatest hindrances and one of the first that needs to be overcome is denial. You cannot deal with what you won't acknowledge exists. Again and again, in various ways, the scripture says: Face facts. If there is no problem, great! If there is, then deal with it. If you are not doing so well on your own, then let God deal with it.

Your Expectations Shape Your Experience

Perhaps one's sense of discontent is affected by one's expectations. If you believe that this world is only "a vale of tears," then you may very well expect to feel miserable, and, since it is your belief that misery is your proper lot, then you will not be motivated to seek a better lot. If you feel that life is "a tale of sound and fury, told by an idiot, signifying nothing," then that belief in meaninglessness would also tend to undercut any desire to improve your lot in life. And there are other styles of belief in meaninglessness and futility that would serve the same purpose.

I submit that the emotional experience of misery itself is a sign of discontent and an argument that one's spirit looks for more. Without going into all the philosophical arguments that could be entailed, I will argue that the Christian position is one of hope. The keystone scripture I have used here, from Jeremiah 6:14, certainly implies that to cry "Peace" when there is no peace is wrong. Thereby, it also implies, I would argue, that the pursuit of "peace" is both good and possible.

While I am a Wesleyan and not in sympathy with all of Calvinist theology, I am very fond of one of its creations, The Westminster Shorter Catechism of 1647. At least, I delight in its opening question and answer. "Question. 1. What is the chief end of man? Answer. Man's chief end is to glorify God and enjoy him forever."

However badly some of us may glorify God, I think most Christians have a fair general grasp of what that means: We are to do good things, and to not do bad things, according to the will of God. That is quite true, and I heartily affirm that. (I acknowledge that I have too narrowly defined "to glorify God," but I trust that this definition will work for the present purpose.) The next element, however, I think some of us grasp far more tentatively. I fear that many, who want to do right and be the best Christians they can be, do not really expect to "enjoy God forever." And some Christians and non-Christians do not expect to enjoy "life," but I submit that life is a sub-category of God, and mankind is intended to enjoy both. Some Christians may expect to enjoy God in the hereafter, but not here and now. I submit that "forever" includes here and now. If my reading is right, then we should generally expect to enjoy God, not only hereafter, but also here and now. If that is so, then if we do *not* enjoy God here and now, then that too is some sign that something is amiss, something is outside of its *intended natural* order, and thereby a prod to seek that enjoyment.

If you suppose that there is no order, then it should follow that there is no *dis*order. Many proclaim such nonsense, but no one actually believes it. If there were really no order, then one could hardly object to any discomfort from "disorder," but in fact, there is an order, God's order. And, generally speaking, every experience of discomfort is a validation that there is an order and that one is out of it. Jesus said that He came so that we might have abundant life (John 10:10), and that He desired to lighten our burdens (Matthew 11:28), and that He wanted to set the captives free (Luke 4:18). All of these verses argue, I submit, that the proper or standard or normal state of life in Christ is to enjoy God forever, beginning now.

In this chapter I argue that we must face facts. The meaning of the facts we face is to be seen in the context of the joy we are supposed to have. If you are not having it, expect to and pursue it.

JIM HILL

Chapter Four: How to Use This Stuff

Whatever you do, work at it with all your heart, as working for the Lord, not for men, since you know that you will receive an inheritance from the Lord as a reward. It is the Lord you are serving.
— Colossians 3:23-24

I will make some further comments about how to use the material following this chapter as I discuss particular principles. I believe that it will make it easier to understand the material to be given if I give the reader some idea of how it is normally employed *before* you read what follows, and therefore, I have placed this here rather than later. I fear there is some risk that this material is not as exciting as what follows. I ask the reader's indulgence. I believe that you will find the potential rewards well worth the effort. There are a number of principles relevant to healing which I believe I have found and have discussed or will. I have already discussed my contentions that effects have causes, that there is a godly order, that God's plans for mankind are for good, and that dealing with reality usually works better than hiding from it. The seven principles which will follow are: 1) We need to get God involved, 2) We need to mourn, 3) We need to forgive, 4) We need to repent, 5) We need to renew the mind, 6) We need to ask Jesus to heal, and 7) We can come to know that God was with us, even in grief, and thus that He is with us now and will be with us in the future as well.

In theory, there is no reason why these principles cannot be applied by individuals alone in prayer with God. I see no theoretical reason why this cannot be done, and I am sure that it can be done successfully sometimes. However, it seems that often we need another. Often, we simply cannot minister to ourselves as we might like. We cannot see ourselves with sufficient clarity, or we need to be able to trust some other in order to deal with some issues. Perhaps God has so designed it so that we are forced to be in relationship, in community. So, while I invite the reader to consider how he or she might put these things to use for him- or herself, I have drawn upon my experience of working with others and, largely, I have stated them in such a framework, and I expect that they will, usually, work best with some other as counselor.

In most cases, when people have come to me to talk about some problem, and we subsequently worked in the light of the principles to be discussed, there was no question that there was a significant problem of one sort or another. Some of the stories shared above have noted some of the presenting problems; there have been many others. One person had trash piling up in her home. She could not get it out. Her family came to clean out her place, and had her get counseling of some sort. Her counselors apparently saw nothing in the trash issue. I thought it likely that she was saying that she had problems in her life that she could not get cleaned up. She was; she did; it was. Others have come with severe physical problems, sometimes with absolutely no idea that there might be a spiritual cause. Others have come presenting lack of sleep, or unwanted attractions, or recurring thoughts of doing things they thought abhorrent. Others had just committed adultery and had marriages in danger, others had a problem with pornography, and others recognized that they were excessively critical. I do not know that it will be hard to recognize that you have a problem if you have one. However, if you are in doubt about the possible applicability of this kind of ministry to a given set of circumstances, you might find the diagnostic tests offered below to be helpful.

It is perfectly alright to *not* have a problem!

It is perfectly alright *not* to have a problem. If that is your circumstance, great! However, if you think that you might have a problem but you are not sure, one preliminary thing that might be done is to ask God. If you are not sure if you have anything on which to work, or what you are to work on, one place to start is to ask God. James 1:5 says, "If any of you lacks wisdom, he should ask God, who gives generously to all without finding fault, and it will be given to him." In John 16:13, Jesus directs us to ask the Holy Spirit to guide us: "But when He, the Spirit of truth, comes, He will guide you into all truth."

If God gives you something very clear and something you think you can easily deal with, great! Then deal with it, and forget the rest of this stuff. But if it is not so easy to work with, or if you cannot make the change you sense is necessary, then ask God to tell you why not.

Most Sins Are Illegitimate Attempts to Get Legitimate Needs Met

As a rule of thumb, most of our sins are attempts to get legitimate needs met by illegitimate means. Trying to quash the bad habit, thought or feeling without finding the real need and finding a legitimate way to meet it, often will not work at all and usually will not work well. Many people are frustrated in their attempts to make significant changes in their lives and in their relationship with God because they prayed for God to change a symptom, but they never got down to a cause. God can certainly ease symptoms for a season. Indeed, perhaps sometimes, radical treatment of symptoms may so change the spiritual environment of a person that even the core person is changed, but note that I said "perhaps" and "sometimes." By far the more sure way to healing is to find causes and to deal with them. In addition, one may very well also have to work on whatever bad habits one may have already developed in response to the underlying or original disturbance.

If what you are doing is not working, you might make some brief review of past problems or traumas to see if that reveals an answer. If that is so, then great again. If not, keep going. If you are still struggling to find something you need to work on, you might try one or more of the four diagnostic tests noted below.

Here Are Four Diagnostic Tests

I propose four diagnostic tests. These can be used by a person before asking help, or they could be used by a helper to help the person begin to determine if they wanted to work in this way, and, if so, to try to sort out where to begin. Now assuming for the moment that you grant the general utility of dealing with reality and the possible utility of looking for possible spiritual origins for ailments, you might then ask how you can begin to get a sense if this is or is not a kind of examination you ought to make. How can I determine if there might be any facts I need to face? I have four diagnostic tests to propose. They are not holy writ, but they should be useful.

Test Number 1: Do You Have a Problem You Cannot Explain?

Jan Frank is an author and lecturer on issues of childhood molestation. She was herself molested in childhood. She thought she had dealt with it. She thought she was healed. Life goes on, and her life went on. She did pretty normal things, including getting married, and was highly functional in many ways. Over time, she noticed that she was awfully hard on her husband. She would be very upset with him over things that were either trifles or were things he simply could not have controlled. After she noticed this, she began to think on it, and eventually she realized that she had taken a vow as a young girl who had been molested by a man that she would never trust a man again. She had a problem she could not explain. She looked for a cause. She found it. It was healed in the spiritual realm.

Test Number 2: Do You Have a Recurring Problem?

There was a woman who came to my church from time to time who managed to get into conflict with nearly everyone she knew at some point in time, including family members and various groups at different churches. One time she got a hold of me in the parking lot and asked me to help her with something. She wanted me to set up a meeting between her and another woman in church with whom she had a conflict. She wanted me to use my authority as pastor to get the other woman to meet with her. They had had many meetings, but I was to see to it that she got to say what she wanted to say, and the other person was not to come on too strong. She also wanted me not to express any opinions; I was not to take sides, since she feared that I might not take her side.

We had talked many times before. We talked for a while in the parking lot. At some point when I felt it was appropriate, I said something like, "You know, as we have spoken at different times, you have reported conflict with nearly everyone you know at some point in time. Do you think it might be something in you? One thing I have found is that when the one common denominator to a series of problems is you, you might be bringing some problem with you. Could that be the case here?" She was quiet for a moment, seemingly considering the point seriously, then she replied, "Well, couldn't it just be that everybody else is wrong?".... I do not know what I answered, or if I did. Yes, I will say now, it *could* possibly be everybody else, but that is highly unlikely, highly unlikely. (By the way, to the best of my knowledge, this person has consumed many hours of caring conversation and counsel by lay and clergy alike, but has not yet seen any correlation between her conduct and her conflicts, and shows no sign of changing, or finding peace, any time soon.)

If you have a problem that keeps coming up in various settings, and with different people, or at different times, then you will want to consider seriously whether or not there is something in you that you are bringing to these situations.

Test Number 3: Do You Find that You Have a Clearly Disproportionate Response to Some Problem or Irritation?

If you fly off the handle for minor irritations, then the minor irritation *may be a trigger, but it is not the reason* for your outburst. If a minor disappointment throws you into great despair, that minor disappointment may well have triggered some hidden but unhealed sense of rejection or expectation of defeat, but it was not the cause of the problem, and the problem will not be healed until you get to the source. A minor criticism, or even a joking one by a friend, may cause us great anger or a renewed sense of failure. When that happens, there is almost surely something deeper which the known event has triggered, but not caused, and it would be well to look for the cause – so that it might be healed.

Test Number 4: Are You Aware of Traumatic Events in Your Past which Might Be the Source of Problems?

Let me add the caution again that you do not need to go looking for trouble when there is no trouble. It is quite alright to cry "Peace" when there is peace. However, if you sense that there is some problem, but you are unable to get a handle on what it is, you might make a survey of past traumatic events as a starting point. Sexual abuse, physical abuse, emotional abuse, abandonment, and severe illness or injury or threatened injury, especially if they happened in childhood when we had no means to understand nor to protect ourselves, are all things likely to set us up for grief. If no specific things come to mind for you, but you did experience one or more of such traumas, then you might try to work through one incident of one such trauma with the pattern I will offer below and see where that leads you. If such traumas have not been dealt with, it is a virtual certainty that they have had consequences in your life and will continue to do so until they are dealt with.

These diagnostic tests are merely means to help you get started in applying one principle I offer: Face facts.

Take Bite Sized Bites

You can deal with five or six different issues, but not all at the same time! As a rule of thumb, jumping from one issue to another is *not* a way to deal with problems; it is a way to *avoid dealing* with problems. It may well be that there is more than one issue to deal with, or that there is more than one truly traumatic incident which needs to be dealt with. Have no fear; they can all be dealt with; but not all at the same time. Deal with one; then deal with another; it will get easier as you go. (Well, it may get harder for a while as you get confidence to deal with increasingly messy stuff, but then it will get easier after a while. And, the net result is worth the effort. And many times, it is much easier than it may sound at the moment.)

Rome Was Not Built in a Day

You did not get to where you are in a day, therefore, you may need more than a day to get from where you are to where you need to be. Sometimes great things happen in short order. Sometimes it is something like peeling an onion, there is often another layer to peel away. Sometimes dealing with X then enables you to deal with Y, which then enables you to deal with Z, and so on. If there has been a great deal of trauma, my experience is that relatively less troubling things may come out first. Successfully dealing with that will enable the counselee to deal with something deeper next, and so on. However, know this: Some help comes immediately. A woman came who had massive trauma to her spirit. One, and only one, of the consequences of her spiritual trauma was that she was continually sick, with cold after flu after bronchitis and so on. *While dealing with all the stuff that needed to be dealt with took a long time, never-the-less from the beginning of the process, the pattern of ongoing sickness abruptly ended.* Expect real benefit.

Spiritual Preparations

Here are some practical suggestions on how to proceed. You need to get yourself, the place where you are meeting, and the other person spiritually set as best you can. When I sense a conversation is going towards dealing with serious matters, I begin to pray silently even as the conversation proceeds. I may have been praying silently during the conversation for some time before the person seeking help has asked for it. Once it is established that we are going to try to deal with something serious, in this case with a spiritual cause of a present affliction, then I do indeed tell them that I am going to pray, and I ask their permission, and I will ask them to make various prayers as well.

We are not the powerful agents in this. God is. This is a spiritual work. God does the work. However, we ask Him to show up. In Jesus' name, I ask God the Father to send his Holy Spirit to come and build a hedge of protection around us and make us entirely secure within whatever space we are. I also ask Him, according to his will, to send angels, rank upon rank, if He pleases, to stand guard, to guide, to do battle or to perform such other tasks as He determines, but most especially do I implore the presence of his Holy Spirit.

[If a reader wishes to employ the principles to follow from a non-Christian perspective, he is welcome to try. Then you will have to make such adjustments in application as seems appropriate to you. I believe that many of the things I shall unfold can be used helpfully in a non-Christian context, though not all, and none so well, but that is yours to determine. Should you find insufficient benefit working from such a perspective, then I heartily encourage you to try "working" from a Christian perspective, that is to say, try putting your faith in Jesus Christ.]

Some of the Work in Prayer

After having attempted to make myself spiritually

fit for the job and then the place where we are at spiritually fit for the work at hand, then I will pray for the person various prayers, and then ask them to pray various prayers of commitment, and then I pray for them again. I have already had the person give me specific permission to pray for them. Then I may plead the blood of Jesus over the person. I may then pray that the Holy Spirit come and indwell the person. I may claim the person, body, soul and spirit for the Lordship of Jesus Christ. Sometimes the person will balk at certain prayers, or will later report different sensations at different parts of the prayer, and this may give some useful information about a sore spot.

At some point after praying a bit for the person, I will ask the one I am counseling to repeat various prayers of commitment to Christ. (Obviously this is a problem for one attempting to work from a non-Christian perspective, and I do not know how to guide you there. Good luck.) I ask them to ask God to be their Heavenly Father, greater than any they have known on earth, and to ask Him to make up any deficits in their fathering or mothering should there have been any. (Many people have had problems with their earthly fathers which have hindered them in their relationship with their heavenly Father, and this aspect of the prayer may begin to open them up to dealing with that.) I ask them to ask Jesus Christ to be Lord of their life, or to acknowledge Him as Lord. I ask them to ask Jesus to be their Savior. I may ask them to say that they do not know all that they need saving from, but they ask Him to save them from all of it. I may ask them to repent of any sins they may have committed "by thought, word or deed, knowingly or unknowingly, sins of the flesh or sins of the spirit." I may ask them to declare that if they ever gave permission for anything evil to enter their life, they now revoke that permission. I ask them to invite the Holy Sprit to come into their lives, into every part of their lives.

I also give persons permission to change the wording in the various prayers of commitment to faith and repentance which I ask them to pray, if they feel a need to. I think that giving them permission to do that diminishes their fear of being manipulated. However, I find that those who feel a need to fine tune every prayer generally do not get much help. They are too tightly wrapped up in their established assumptions to receive anything new.

Once they have prayed for themselves, I may then pray on their behalf, claiming the authority to do so which they have given me, and claiming the authority their own prayers of commitment have just given in the spiritual realm, and based upon the authority which I have in Christ. At this point I would pray against any unholy vows, dedications or consecrations. I would pray against any curses coming to them from the third or fourth generation of either their father's or their mother's line, or unto any generation yet having effect upon them, and against any curse coming to them from any source, declaring them null and void, in Jesus' name or "in the name of the Father and of the Son and of the Holy Spirit." At that point I might command any unclean spirits to leave them and go to the feet of Jesus for his disposition or, if they will not accept that, to be bound and go to the abyss to await the judgment of God at the end of time. The things that follow may serve well without all these prayers, but they will serve better with them.

Ask the Holy Spirit to Guide

Once we have prepared ourselves - the counselor, the place and the counselee - spiritually for the task at hand, then I ask the counselee to tell me what they think we should work on today. I would probably have done that at the start of the session. If we had not done that, then we might use some of the previously discussed diagnostic questions here, or I might simply short-circuit that process by asking the Holy Spirit to speak to their Spirit and bring to mind something that we are to work on at that time.

As noted above, one man had just had a nasty episode of adultery which was very hurtful to his wife, and which he deeply regretted. He felt very badly. He did not know why he would do such a hurtful thing. He could not think of a place to start. I asked God to bring something to mind for him. Before long, he recalled a time when he, as a young child, was lying on the floor watching TV. His older brother came up to him and engaged in play which he should not have. The man's relations with women were ever after influenced by his need to prove that he was a man and not the fit object of penetration which his older brother's actions had seemed to say. My point at the moment is that this man did not know where to begin; nor did I. I asked the Holy Spirit to reveal something relevant, and He did. In my experience, this revelation or recall of a significant event is something that almost always happens, and therefore, I recommend asking the Holy Sprit to bring to the mind of the one seeking help what we are to work on as a way to begin.

Ways to Avoid "Planting" Memories

Some may well be anxious about "planting" memories. You should be, but there are ways to avoid doing that. One of them is that I do very little to suggest what the other sees. I ask God to tell them something, and then I repeatedly ask them to tell me what they see; I do not tell them what to see. I allow them time, and I am in no hurry. If I need to suggest some possibility in order to get needed information or to move along a temporarily slowed conversation, I will ask questions offering multiple possible answers, even if I am sure what the answer is. I will also keep a tone of voice that is matter-of-fact: not surprised, not upset, not judgmental, and trying not to lead to any particular answer.

An Introductory Overview

Now, once we have a specific incident to work with, then ...

1) I get them to give me a little detail, just to be sure that they have something specific in mind.

2) Then I ask them to apply all the principles I have discussed in prayer. I ask them to talk to God.

3) I ask them to mourn, to tell God how much it hurt and how wrong it was.

4) I ask them to forgive the perpetrator.

5) Then I ask them, again talking out loud to God, to repent of any misdeeds of theirs, particularly those related somehow to this spiritual trauma.

6) Then I ask them to repent of wrong thoughts and ask Jesus to renew their minds with biblical truth. (Such as "I repent of believing that I was worthless since I was treated in the way I was, and I affirm that I am a child of God." I give this illustration only so that you will have some idea of what I am talking about.)

7) Then I will ask them to ask God to heal them.

8) After that, I may ask them to recall the scene once more, and then to tell me what they can see in the spiritual realm. I do *not* do imagery exercises. I do not ask them *to see*, but I ask them *if* they *can see* anything in the spiritual realm. I *do* ask them to look; I *do not* ask them to imagine. In my experience, the counselee will almost always, though not quite always, see something which is profoundly helpful. Each of these steps is discussed in more detail in a following chapter.

My main point here, is that, and least for all but the last step, they are doing these things (mourn, repent, forgive, *etcetera*) in prayer to God.

I have asked them to pray out loud so that I can monitor what they are doing. I may not know how honestly and thoroughly they have processed things unless I can hear them. I want them to do the praying, so that they are doing the work and not I.

I *may* pray on their behalf in some of these areas, in order to help them along if they seem to have a hard time of putting their thoughts and feelings into words, but it must be *their* thoughts and feelings you express. *If* you are going to pray on the other's behalf it is *very* important that, while trying to pray what should be prayed, you pray their own thoughts and feelings honestly. It is better to leave some work undone (to be done another time) than to do it falsely. To pray for them falsely is to leave it undone and to mask that fact. You may try to nudge them in the right direction a bit, but you cannot take over for them. That just isn't real, and, in my experience, it just doesn't work. For example, if they are not ready to forgive, do not say it for them and assume that it is done; it isn't. At that point, you might ask them if they could say, "Lord, help me want to forgive," or some thing you think both moves in the right direction and is true to their feelings.

Does that mean that sometimes you cannot get the results that are possible because a person is unwilling to do what they need to do? Yes, absolutely. You are not God. Don't try to be. You can lead a horse to water, you can talk about how helpful the water might be, you can commiserate with them by talking about the time you had a hard time taking a sip of water yourself as an encouragement to the horse, but you cannot make the horse drink. At some point, the horse has got to drink on his own. If you are the horse, I hope you have a big, long drink and that you find it very refreshing. If you are the one helping the horse, I hope you can lead them to water well and that they then drink fully and freely and to great benefit.

I have seen the things of which I have spoken work, many times. I know they can be of value. I find that we are made in a certain way, and that God does have words to tell us about how to repair our wounded spirits when something is amiss. I find that we are all messed up in some ways; after all, that is one of the things implied by Paul in Romans 3:23 ("For all have sinned and fall short of the glory of God." – Romans 3:23). I find that many of our problems have had origins we have forgotten, or, perhaps, *never consciously knew*. I find that there are spiritual origins for many physical ailments, and social ailments, and emotional ailments, and their practical consequences in our lives. Since there are spiritual origins, it is reasonable to suspect that there might be spiritual cures. I find that to be true also. I believe that God wants us to be whole and healthy; after all, surely that is what Jesus is telling us in John 10:10 ("I have come that they may have life, and have it to the full."). Anything less is sub-standard. I do not want you to settle for a sub-standard life, for yourself or for others. These things I offer as a means, within God's gracious economy, to find healing, release, forgiveness, freedom, peace, joy, strength, and increasing ability to love and an increasing ability to receive love.

Chapter Five: We Need Not Just Godly Principles, But God

Jesus answered, "I am the way and the truth and the life. No one comes to the Father except through me. If you really knew me, you would know my father as well. From now on, you do know him and have seen him."
- Jesus, in John 14:6-7

Bear with me; the point of this story comes at the end. It was one of the earliest times that I was asked to deliver someone of an unclean spirit. She was eighteen years old. She came to my office to ask me to "cast a demon out of her" – her language, not mine, but accurate enough. I talked to her about diet, exercise, rest, and medicines – in short, about any possible natural things I could think of that might be a factor in the problems she felt she had. After an hour of this dance, she said that no, those things were not the problem. She had an unclean spirit in her. She thought she knew where it came from. And she wanted it out.

We sat on opposites sides of the room. I prayed, commanding any unclean spirit to leave in Jesus' name. There were signs of struggle. After a season, she said, "There; it left. I felt toes on the top of my head as it left." (Do not jump to too many conclusions. This is what happened on this occasion, not all the time.) She paused for a moment to assess how she felt, and then she said, "Wow, for the first time in my life I am not filled with anger and hatred."

She did not come to church right after that, so I went to visit her with the family she was staying with. The grandmother of that family said to me, "I don't know what you did, but the difference is night and day. She was impossible to get along with before, but now she is sweet and helpful." I did not do anything; whatever was done was done by Jesus; but I tell you this so that you will know that the change was real and substantial.

When the girl had first come to the office, she had asked about being baptized. However, we never got back to that during that visit. We got caught up in her quest to be delivered. ("Deliverance ministry" is what casting out unclean spirits is usually called among Protestants.) Our session had lasted about an hour and a half, which I thought was a long time at the time (I have had much longer sessions since then.); so, I was ready to call it quits. The results were spectacular, and I was sure that she would be back in church every time the doors were open after that experience. So I was confident that we would have plenty of opportunity for her to make a clear commitment to Christ and to get her baptized. Wrong. You recall that I visited her because she did not come back to church right away. Well, she never did. And some months later she fell into major sin, causing a great deal of anguish for the family with whom she had been living. From that time, I decided that I never wanted to have a significant ministry session with anyone without giving them an opportunity to make a commitment to Christ. I urge you to find out if your counselee is in Christ, and, if not, to give them an opportunity to enter into a relationship with Jesus Christ. (This should make perfect sense for my Christian readers, but may be a bit off-putting for my non-Christian readers. You will have to do with it whatever you can.)

In chapter 20, verses 30-31, John gives us the reason that he wrote his gospel: "Jesus did many other miraculous signs in the presence of his disciples, which are not recorded in this book. But these are written that you may believe that Jesus is the Christ, the Son of God, and that by believing you may have life in his name."

I share John's two expressed concerns. I too want you to have life, full life, abundant life, joyful life. I also believe that Jesus is the Christ, the Son of God, and that this life is to be found in Jesus' name, and I hope that reading some of the things in this book will lead the reader to see that there is power for new life in Jesus' name.

The day of Pentecost and Peter's first proclamation of the Christian gospel is recorded in Acts 2. Many were touched by what he said and asked what they should do in response. Here is the question and the answer given in verses 37-38: "When the people heard this they were cut to the heart and said to Peter and the other apostles, 'Brothers, what shall we do.' Peter replied, 'Repent and be baptized, every one of you, in the name of Jesus Christ for the forgiveness of your sins. And you will receive the gift of the Holy Spirit.'"

The Holy Sprit is central to what we do in this kind of ministry. God *does* hear the prayers of those who do not believe in Him, but the one who believes in God knows better what to pray and hears God's reply far more readily and has access to a power that the one who does not know God does not so readily have.

In John 6, Jesus was asked what must one do to do the works that God requires. He answered, as recorded in verse 29: "The work of God is this: to believe in the one he has sent."

Again, for my Christian readers, this should all make perfect sense and I am already gilding the lily. For my non-Christian readers, I do not know what you are to make of this. I would be delighted should you also come to make a commitment to Christ. I invite you to continue to read and to see what sense the pieces make when put together. You are, of course, to use them as makes sense to you.

As for the efficacy of the following principles in the absence of a commitment to Christ, will they work? Yes, of course. If God has made all people, as Christian faith says He has, and if He knows how we are made, as Christian faith says He does, then it would seem to follow that He might very well have made us according to spiritual principles that work even if we do not acknowledge the source from which they came. God made gravity, and gravity "works" whether you acknowledge its origins in God or not. So do the spiritual principles I will unfold. However, having said that, I think that these principles and procedures will tend to work less well, especially when they rely upon the agency of the Holy Spirit or the authority of Jesus' name to achieve their effect, as they often do. Furthermore, as my opening story in this chapter should suggest, the security of the benefit obtained is far, far greater when one is secure in Christ than when one is not.

Chapter Six: Mourning is God's Road to Comfort

Blessed are those who mourn, for they will be comforted.
– Matthew 5:4

I am dumbfounded by the Christian people who say there is no place in Christian faith for mourning, and there are a lot of them. First, let me quote you what Jesus said: "Blessed are those who mourn for they shall be comforted." [Matthew 5:4] Many people who call themselves Christians consider that the words of Jesus are authoritative. Apparently, others do not. By the way, He said this in the Sermon on the Mount, which is often considered one of the better known and more exalted collections of his teaching. I submit that this statement alone is sufficient to gain a place for the argument that there is a place for mourning in life. However, there is much more in scripture to support this concept of mourning. Let me note some of it and then I will come back and explain further what Jesus said here and how it can be helpful.

Mourning Is Biblical:

I have never surveyed all the psalms, but I know that psalms 2, 3, 4, 5, 6 and 7, all begin as laments. Psalm 22 is one of the most famous of laments ever: "My God, my God, why hast Thou forsaken me?" I would hazard the guess that about half the psalms are laments, or rather begin as laments. They do not end that way. If there is that much lamentation in the Psalms, does that suggest that there may be a place for it in life? It is an amazing thing that when you take your hurts to God, when you honestly pour out your heart to Him, He does something strange: He changes your heart. I think there is only one of the psalms, out of all that begin with lament, that does not end in triumph and praise.

Psalm 22 is a good example of godly mourning. Christ quoted it on the cross. "My God, my God, why hast Thou forsaken me?" the psalmist asks. David was caught up in despair a thousand years before Christ. After two verses, he recalls that God has been active to protect and bless the community of faith for centuries before, in verses 3-5. Then, in verses 6-9, he is caught up again in his own misery, rejection and despair. In verses 9-10, he recalls his own personal experience of God's blessing presence in his life. In verse 11, he makes a plea for help. In verses 12 through 18, he is overwhelmed by the abuse he is then receiving. (By the way, there is an absolutely amazing fulfillment of very specific elements of this psalm in the crucifixion of Jesus Christ, a psalm that was written a thousand years before that crucifixion). In verses 19 through 21, once again he is moved to ask for God's help, in a litany that increases in intensity. Then from verse 22 to the end at verse 31, he declares ..., he who began in utter despair,... he declares that he will proclaim to a generation yet unborn the righteousness of God, and his last shout is this: "He has done it." (Take a look at John 19:30 sometime. Jesus proclaimed on the cross that "It is finished," or "I have done it.") Here a man began in despair, but ended in exultation. But that, dear hearts, is what happens when you mourn as God would have us mourn. With one exception, if I recall correctly, all of the psalms that begin in lament end in triumph.

I kept a journal in verse for a year shortly after I came to Christ as an adult. I brought to it whatever I had to say. Often, my poems began as laments, very often.

But very rarely did they end that way. That is what I find happens when you deal honestly with God. God changes your heart. The "problem" may not be solved, the circumstances may not be changed, but your attitude is changed, and you no longer have despair, but joy! That is the purpose of mourning, to get release from sorrow. (By the way, before I leave the scriptural evidence, let me note that there is also a whole book of the Bible called Lamentations. What do you think that is about? Then too, you will not want to overlook Ecclesiastes 3:1 and 4, at least not if you actually want to be in accord with scripture rather than your preconceived theologies. "There is a time for everything, and a season for every activity under heaven: A time to weep, and a time to laugh, and a time to mourn and a time to dance.")

What Mourning Is, What It Is Not

Jesus did *not* say that it is good to have a reason to mourn, but he said that *when you have a reason to mourn, it is good to do it*. The reader should re-read that last sentence: It notes a key distinction. The virtue is *not* in having a reason to mourn, *but* in *doing the mourning when you do have a reason.*

Have you ever heard the phrase: "To have a good cry"? What do you suppose that is about? How can a cry be good? Because on the other side of crying there is release!

For some twenty-five years, I have taken people in need into my home. Some of the young men have become as sons to me. One of them who had become a son to me apparently killed his wife and killed himself when she said she was going to leave him. That was as painful an event in my life as I can recall. For a couple of weeks after their deaths, whenever anybody hugged me or said the word "love," I would feel great pain and cry. This pain was physical pain; I do not know anything about "emotional pain." And it hurt when I cried. But after I cried, I felt better. Somehow I was crying *through* the pain. It was a part of my mourning. I did not hide from the emotions, or from people. People came and sat with me during this time; we talked of many things. While I had another pastor preside at the memorial service, I also spoke at that service, drawing what lessons I could and dealing with the painful realities. Easter Sunday came shortly thereafter, and I faced all the awkward and painful facts at the Easter services. Deep hurts are not fully dealt with in a moment, and they may leave some residue for years, or longer, but, for health's sake, they can and should be substantially dealt with, or processed, or worked through, or grieved, or mourned. The purpose of mourning is to get through grief. "Blessed are those who mourn, *for they shall be comforted.*" The purpose of mourning is comfort.

I think this is very much like what is commonly called, in other settings, the grief process. Many times people try to sweep their emotions under the rug. Then they discover that they trip over lumps in the rug and they do not know why. They need to clean out their rugs. You can get *through* the pain but you cannot jump *over* it. The jumpers don't quite make it. Oh, they may live, but not as fully, and perhaps not ever again.

Mourning is not a place to set up camp, but it is a place to go through. Indeed, if you find that you are stuck in permanent grief, it may well be that you have never properly mourned.

Why You May Not Have Mourned

Now then, when something awful has happened to you as a child, you may never have had a chance to mourn. You may not even have known if you *should* feel bad! After all, you only know what goes on in your own family, and you do not know if this is normal or not; you only know something feels bad. Furthermore, it may well be that the perpetrators of your injury have charge over you, and it simply was not safe to mourn. You feared that you would be hurt worse if you did. The perpetrators of your injury may also be those who give you food and shelter and other indications of genuine love and affection. You may be confused about what good and bad or right and wrong means. If the hurts were severe and untreated, then you may have suppressed the memories. It can also be the case that things which might not be particularly consequential for one child are powerful for another. It might be that things you came to believe were normal childhood or adolescent games between peers or between younger children and older children, and therefore, in your mind, should not have been the source of trouble, did in fact have far greater consequences than you realized. For a variety of reasons, you may have had enormous hurts churning deep inside you for decades. That is not healthy.

While childhood is often the place where such things first arise, there can be trauma to the spirit at any time in life. In childhood, we have the least ability to understand things, and we have the least power to respond to things, and we are the most dependent and the most vulnerable. For that reason, many of the deepest wounds of the spirit will often be found to have had origins in childhood. However, life-threatening accidents, life-threatening illness, rape and other traumatic events can very well cause us similar grief as adolescents, as young adults, and at any age as adults. *Furthermore, it is likely that if we have been wounded in childhood in some way, and those events have not been dealt with, we are more likely to be wounded again in the course of our life.* Additionally, it may well be that a more recent and less traumatizing issue may be the first that is brought to mind since it may not be as overwhelming as an earlier event. As we work through one issue and get some healing, then we are able to go on to another, more troubling issue.

How We Work This Step

With each step, I ask the counselee to pray to God and to pray out loud. I ask them to pray out loud so that I may have some understanding of what progress they are making in dealing with their issues. In the step of mourning, I want them primarily to tell God two things: 1) What was wrong with it and 2) How bad it was. All the expressions of hurt they never could get out before, I want them to get out now. In so far as they are able, it is appropriate to attach all the bad consequences they can see related to this bad event also. For example, perhaps a woman was molested and she later concluded that she was of little worth and gave herself to many men: That later sense of worthlessness and promiscuity she now hates she should acknowledge too. If the harmful act was a betrayal of trust, complain of that too. All these feelings are there; the point here is to bring them out so that God can deal with them.

More Hindrances to Mourning

Another problem I often find with Christians arises from their mistaken notion of perfection. Others can have this problem too; for them it simply arises from their unacknowledged "theology." People want to censor their remarks. They want them to be tidy, pretty, inoffensive, noble, and "correct." To that I say, what rubbish. This is not the time for that. There is a time for that; this is not it. If you have been hurt, it is appropriate to acknowledge your pain. If somebody did you wrong, it is okay to say that somebody did you wrong. Realize that this is just between you and God, and maybe a counselor; and if your counselor cannot be trusted to keep his mouth shut and also to know when to ignore what you say, dump him.

Now if you were a parent, and let us assume that you are a very good parent, and your young child comes to you crying, with some severe injury, are you going to backhand him across the room and tell him to shut up? I trust not. Well, what on God's green earth makes you think that you are more noble than God? More gracious than God? More loving than God? If you would not do that to your child, can you not trust that God will not do that to you?

You see, the important thing here is for you to begin to deal with whatever it is that has crippled your soul all these years. And if that means you need to go through a few misstatements or a little theological error (provided that you are trying to be as honest as you can be) or use some non-genteel language, that is okay for now. Yes, we do not want to accuse anyone unjustly, and you should always avoid that. Yes, you do not want to make *any* theological errors, and you try to avoid that, and, if need be, you or your counselor should clean that up later. Foul language is never what you want to use and generally should be avoided. But none of those things are the most pressing issue at the moment when you are mourning, especially when you are mourning a loss you have not acknowledged for many years. God will not (at least not generally) deal with a hurt you will not let go of, you will not hand over to Him. And you have got to have the freedom you need to blurt out the pains you may have suppressed for many years.

If anyone uses the preceding statements about

God's grace as an excuse to willfully slander man or God or willfully offend others, you have just shot yourself in the foot, and you will very likely *not* get healing. However, if you are merely being sloppy in the midst of pain, fine; God can deal with that, and you can clean up your act later. Some of the things I sometimes tell people are that: God is a tough old bird. He's been around a long time, you know. He has probably seen it before. You are not going to shock Him. And, if you are being as honest as you can be, you are not going to offend Him. It is important that you get out what is really bothering you so that God can begin to help you heal.

Another problem people have is that they are in an awful hurry, and they want to jump to steps two, and three and so on, without really going through step one. Augustine said: *Festina lente*, which means "Make haste slowly." John Wooden used to say, "Be quick, but don't hurry." My mother used to say, "Haste makes waste." People are often unable to say that a perpetrator did wrong because they "know" that as Christians they have to "forgive" him. True enough, but if they had really been able to do that, they probably would not now be in need of help! So, please, know that we are going to forgive others as need be, all others as need be, and self too if need be, but just now let us deal with the mourning.

Other people may want to rush on to their own repentance. They know that they need to repent, which is true enough, and so they do not want to give any time to this namby-pamby, self-indulgent mourning stuff. They can take it on the chin. So let's take our responsibility and repent. We will just tell God how sorry we feel, and that should take care of it. Wrong. First, if they are inclined to do that, they have probably already done that and it did not work or they would not be asking for help, and continuing to do what does not work is one definition of insanity. Second, we will get to the repentance in time, rest assured. We will do all the repenting you need, including some you may not yet know you need, but now is the time for mourning. Third, this rush to repentance is often *not* so much an expression of responsibility taking as it is of a desire to avoid the pain of mourning - and that is why we have to go through it. You *can* work *through* the pain; you *cannot jump over* it.

Mourning: Tell God how wrong it was and how much it hurt, with all the ramifications you can think of, and include expressions of your hurt about all the wrongdoers who were a part of this particular incident that you can think of.

Chapter Seven: Forgiveness Is the Road to Freedom

Forgive us our trespasses as we forgive those who trespass against us.
  – Jesus, quoted in Matthew 6:12,
    in the Lord's Prayer
For if you forgive men when they sin against you,
your heavenly Father will also forgive you.
But if you do not forgive men their sins, your Father
will not forgive your sins.
  – Matthew 6:14

This is perhaps one of the best known hallmarks of the Christian perspective. Christians are mocked by some for it. God Himself has been mocked by "clever intellectuals" for it. Heinrich Heine said, among his last words, "Bien sûr, il me pardonnera; c'est son métier." ("Of course, he [God] will pardon me; it is his profession.") Many persons trade upon the assumption that forgiveness will be granted to them easily, indulging themselves in evil in the expectation that it will not be taken seriously.

Many Christians rush to declare a forgiveness they are not ready to give, and have not; and others let themselves be inappropriately vulnerable, believing that forgiveness requires it. Forgiveness is necessary. It may or may not be helpful to the one who is forgiven. It is profoundly helpful to the one who forgives. It is necessary for the one who has been injured to forgive for the sake of his eternal health. It is often misunderstood.

"I Won't Forgive Him If It Kills Me!"

The metaphors in ordinary language are often colorful and, when examined, insightful. Imagine this: A person has been deeply offended or injured or hurt by someone. He or she is understandably upset. He is angry. His blood pressure rises, his pulse quickens, his breathing is more labored; he seethes. And in this mood, he says, "I won't forgive him (the perpetrator). I won't forgive him if it kills me."

You have heard it before: "I won't forgive him/her if it kills me." On one level, it is a declaration that the injury was perceived as so grave that the injured party will not ever forgive the injurer, no matter what the cost.

But the obvious implication is that the cost could be that of the unforgiving person's life. In some way, the English language community has sensed that unforgiveness does have serious consequences, and that it just might kill you.

As a matter of physiology that is a very sound insight. The attitude of unforgiveness leads to a state of constant vigilance. This state of constant vigilance, being always in the flight-fight mode, has physiological consequences. It is a perfectly healthy response to sudden threats, but to sustain this attitude affects the body chemistry in ways that will break down the immune system over time and have other physical health consequences that are bad. Unforgiveness can kill you. It may not do it over night. It may take years. But it will get you. And in the meantime, you will have years of misery.

God does not tell us to do things because He is some sort of cosmic spoil-sport who just tries to keep us from having any fun. If God tells us to do something, there is good reason for it, and it is for our good. When He tells us to forgive, that too is because it is good for us. Unforgiveness will harden your spiritual heart and it will harden your physical arteries. Forgiveness is necessary, but it is sometimes misunderstood. Let us see if we can come to understand it better.

What Forgiveness Is Not

To forgive a person's act does *not* mean that what they did was not wrong. You *only* forgive things that are wrong! If someone you did not know came up to you and gave you a wonderful gift, you would not say to them, "I forgive you." You would say, "For me? Wow, thanks," or something like it. Anytime one person says they forgive another, it means that they believe that the other has wronged them. Have you not seen that sometimes people are angry with another person's words declaring forgiveness for them because they know it implies a declaration of wrongdoing and they are not prepared to acknowledge wrongdoing? Forgiveness does not mean it was not wrong; it means it was.

Forgiveness does not mean it did not matter. The more it mattered the more difficult it may be to forgive, but once again you hardly need to deal with things that did not matter. The more it matters, the harder it may be, and also, probably, the more necessary!

Have you ever tossed and turned all night because of a perceived slight? Have you ever had your concentration on something you wanted to do destroyed by anger or upset over some perceived injury? Have you ever found yourself fearing to go into some social setting because of some unresolved conflict over some perceived injury? In each situation, who was troubled by it? You. You were the one who lost sleep. You were the one who could not concentrate on your work or your play or having fun with the people you were with. You were the one filled with anxiety because you might meet the one with whom you were angry. The purpose of forgiveness is to be set free from that. It will sometimes also be enormously helpful to the other person; occasionally it can be life-transforming; but the clear beneficiary is you. You need to forgive.

In my experience it is often much easier to forgive *after* you have done what I have called mourning. If you have never called wrong, wrong, if you have never declared the injury and damage received (assuming it is a matter of some consequence), then you probably will not really be able to forgive. You may say the words, but you may very well not have done the deed. That is one of the reasons why I deal with mourning before forgiveness.

If the matter is a trifle, then it may well be very easy to deal with. If it is a trifle and it is not easy to deal with, then it may be that it is not the primary issue but only a trigger of a more troubling matter. If the matter is of some consequence, then you will probably have a need to vent, to express your hurt and anger. It *may* be possible and helpful to do that to the perpetrator. However, there are times when it will simply not be possible to do that.

It may be helpful if the wrongdoer can be confronted. If you could speak of your hurt and injury with the one whom you believed injured you, you might discover things about the event that would make it easier to deal with, possibly even change its meaning. If the perpetrator could express sorrow, regret and repentance and ask forgiveness, that might be enormously helpful. However, in most of the situations I have been called upon to work with, that is simply not possible. The perpetrator is dead, or is out of the person's life, or is too old and infirm to be confronted. While reconciliation is helpful and desirable and should be sought when possible, it simply is not always possible, but forgiveness still is, and forgiveness is still necessary.

To Forgive Is Not Necessarily To Trust

Forgiveness does not necessarily mean the restoration of trust. That is a separate matter. I suppose forgiveness would usually mean that *you might be open* to a restoration of trust if the other were truly repentant and that were established and if, over time, trust were restored, but the restoration of trust is a separate issue. If someone has molested you, and you confront him/her, and he/she says he/she repents, that does not mean that you need to act immediately as if nothing has happened, nor put yourself in a position of risk. The specifics of the process of the restoration of trust vary enormously, depending upon what the injury was. Sometimes it will be appropriate for there to be a swift restoration of trust. In many of the situations I have been called upon to deal with in the use of this pattern for the healing of spiritual wounds, the wounds were long ago, and the possibility of a restoration of trust was limited. I have also been called upon to deal with people where there were current injuries in a relationship, and there was confrontation, and there was repentance, and the relatively swift and thorough restoration of trust was entirely appropriate. My point here is that forgiveness does not *necessarily* mean the restoration of trust, and the inability to have such restoration does *not* eliminate the need for forgiveness.

What Forgiveness Is

What on earth does it mean, then? Here is something of what it means. In Deuteronomy 32:35, Moses said, speaking God's words for Him, "It is mine to avenge; I will repay." Paul has this in mind as he speaks in Romans 12:17-19: "Do not repay anyone evil for evil. Be careful to do what is right in the eyes of everybody. If it is possible, as far as it depends on you, live at peace with everyone. Do not take revenge, my friends, but leave room for God's wrath, for it is written: 'It is mine to avenge; I will repay,' says the Lord."

You may recall the words of Jesus in the Sermon on the Mount that say: "Do not judge, or you too will be judged. For in the same way you judge others, you will be judged, and with the measure you use, it will be measured to you." [Matthew 7:1-2] Lest some be misled to think that we are to be hapless, clueless and valueless, know that the Greek word translated "judge" here can reasonably be translated "judge" or "condemn." In John 7:24, Jesus tells people to "stop judging by mere appearances, and make a right judgment." This indicates that we are to "judge" in the sense of discerning right and wrong. In Philippians 1:10, Paul also indicates that discernment is good and necessary. Therefore, I submit that the point here is that we are not to have a condemning spirit. We are to leave ultimate judgment to God. We surrender vengeance to God, or else it comes not only out of the hide of the other, but out of our own.

You are not God. You do not know all. You are not designed to play God. Neither our knowledge nor our understanding is sufficient to exercise vengeance, nor are we well equipped to handle the strain of vengeance. Leave vengeance to God. Surrender judgment to God.

You know right from wrong. In so far as we are able, we make determinations about right and wrong acts, but we attempt to leave ultimate judgment about people to God.

To be sure, we may have responsibilities as police, prosecutors, or judges or as supervisors, teachers, or coaches or simply as parents or even as general members of society to make judgments about the actions of people and to be an agent of reward or punishment, but in that we are exercising a responsibility as best we can, we do not presume that we are God. To forgive does not necessarily mean that we try to let the perpetrator escape punishment. It may be necessary for him to receive consequences for his actions; it may be necessary for the order of society that a perpetrator be punished; or we may simply be too close to render even human judgment in a given case. I am talking about the attitude we need to have towards those who have done us harm. At some point we need to be able to turn them over to God, to surrender punishment to Him, and to not hold thoughts of vengeance towards them in our hearts. And this is for our benefit, not his. Yes, it may benefit the other, and enormously, but it is absolutely necessary for you, for your health, both spiritual and physical.

You May Need to Forgive Yourself

Sometimes you may need to "forgive" yourself. This may not be what is really happening. It may be that what you properly need is to accept God's forgiveness, but it will feel like you need to forgive yourself. And then, sometimes, that is exactly what you need to do. Why not? Are you prefect? Are you the only one who has escaped the human condition? Are you not also included in Romans 3:23: "All have sinned and fall short of the glory of God"? Are you so much worse a sinner than the thief on the cross next to Jesus who asked and received pardon? [See Luke 23:42-43.] Did not Jesus die for your sins as well? Do you disdain the grace of God? If need be, forgive yourself, or ask God's forgiveness and accept it.

You May Need to "Forgive" God

Sometimes you may need to "forgive" God. Now this is simply wrong theologically. God did no wrong, therefore, He has done nothing for which you should forgive Him. However, it may *feel* that way to you at some point in time. Consequently, to *say* something like you "forgive God" may be helpful as a way station, on the way to peace with God. By the time you have worked through all the steps I outline in this book, including the one about finding God in your grief, you will probably want to repent of any such thought and will be freely able to thank God for his presence in your life. However, if you are experiencing anger towards God, and even though that feeling arises from a misunderstanding of the spiritual reality, "forgiving" God *may* be a helpful intermediate step on your path to restoring your relationship with God, and God is big enough and gracious enough to be able to handle your "forgiveness." If you find that you are mad at God, try "forgiving" Him. At some point, I think you will find that silly, and at that point you will move from wanting to forgive God to asking God to forgive you, but it *may* be a useful way station.

Once Is Not Always Enough

You may have to forgive some human perpetrators more than once. You may need to work your way towards forgiveness. You may start out with a grudging request to God for Him to help you *want* to forgive So-and-so, or even with a grudging declaration that you sense that God wants you to do that but that you cannot quite do that yet. You do need to forgive. If you have to work at it, that is okay, but keep working at it, until you have done it. You see, the measure you give is the measure you get back, in more ways than one. Know that you can forgive and you need to forgive and that God has forgiveness for you.

JIM HILL

Chapter Eight: Repentance Is a Good Thing: It's a Do-Over

"The time has come," he said. "The kingdom of God is near. Repent and believe the good news!"
– Jesus, quoted in Mark 1:15

I think I heard some readers say, when they first saw that this chapter dealt with repentance, "Ah, finally we might be getting to some real meat." I think I heard other readers saying, "Oh, and he seemed like such a nice fellow and now he's going to spoil it all." And I think that both groups are mistaken; first, in what they expect of me, and second, in what they should expect of God.

Repentance Is a Blessing, Not a Curse

Repentance is a good thing. Oh, it may be a bit awkward when you *have to* repent, but it is a great relief, release and blessing that you *can repent*. I think many people have a horrible feeling about "repentance." They see a condemning preacher shake his finger at them and declare their need for repentance, implying, in their mind at least, that the preacher claims that he has it all together and that they do not. Worse than that, they feel it implies *not merely* that they have *done* wrong, but that *they are wrong*, that the very core of their being is wrong, and that is intolerable. Well, some preachers may imply that, and some may even believe it, but that is *not* what biblical repentance is about!

Imagine in golf if, when you hit a bad drive you could take the shot over, and not have to count the stroke, would that be a good thing? What about if you make a real mess of things financially, is it a good thing to be able to declare bankruptcy and to start over? That is what repentance is about. It's a "do-over." Yes, it is an "I got to," but even more it is an "I get to." Do you see the difference? You *get* to start over. You *get* to change course. You have an opportunity to change a course that is not right.

Suppose you are going down the freeway and you miss your turnoff, is it a good thing that you can get off at the next exit and get back on the freeway heading the other way and still make your exit? Or do you think it would be better if, whenever you missed your turnoff, you had to stay on the wrong course for ever? What's wrong with changing course when your course is wrong? Suppose you put way too much salt in the water the last time you made rice, and your mouth puckered up because it was so salty, is it okay to do it differently the next time? What's wrong with changing the way you do something when the way you did it before did not work? Yes, it may be awkward to admit we did something wrong, but so what? We are suffering the consequences anyway. Isn't it better to change course and get new consequences than to keep the course and keep the bad consequences of the bad course? Are you going to keep making really bad rice just because you did it wrong the first time and you do not want to admit you did it wrong?

Turn Back, O Man, Just Means Turn Around

The Hebrew word often translated "repent" in the Old Testament is *shub*. It means "turn," or "turn around," or, more figuratively, "change course." It focuses on a change of conduct, based, it is to be understood, upon a change of heart. The Greek word often translated "repent" in the New Testament is *metanoia*. "Meta" means "with" or "after," and "noia" means "mind." The point here is to have a change of mind or attitude so heartfelt that it leads to a change of conduct. Our English words comes from Latin roots that take after the Greek word. "Re" means "again," and "pent" is from a word meaning "to think." Theoretically, a "penitentiary" is a place where people go to think about their deeds or lives. Someone who is "pensive" is in deep thought. So our word "repent" means to rethink something in so deep a way that it leads to both a change of attitude and a change of conduct. But Jesus said more than "repent" in this verse.

The Time Has Come

First He said "the time has come." So then there may have been times when the time had not yet come. And could it be that there are still times when the time has not yet come? Or is it rather the case that now, now that Jesus has come, "the time" has always come? Is it the case that once you know about Jesus, the time has come? Is it the case that now that you know there are causes for problems, the time has come to face them? Could it be that now that you know more things can be healed than you had supposed the time has come to get healed? Yes, I think, to all of the above.

There Is an Answer

Then He said "the kingdom of God is near," or "the kingdom of God is at hand," or "the kingdom of God is right here." Was He talking about himself? Was He talking about a spiritual reality which He represented? Yes, to both. But he was also saying that what people had been looking for was right there? What summarized all earthly hope and fulfillment was at hand? All that man most desired was available? Yes, again.

And now then, since now the time had come and since now there was something good to turn to - the Kingdom of God - now was the time to repent, which means "turn around," in a way that might not have made sense before. It seems that the call to repentance is predicated upon there being something better to turn to, and now that was in place, and indeed right before them. Yes, I think that is so. I mentioned before that we often dare not even acknowledge consciously that we have a problem if we sense there is no way we can deal with it.

Surely the call to repentance can be heard more gladly when it is conjoined with a declaration that there is something far better to turn to. And yet there is more.

There Is Good News for Us

Then Jesus says, "repent and believe the good news." He has good news to tell us. There is healing for us. There is an end to our pain. There can be an end to our crummy behaviors and foul thoughts. There can be an end to guilt and shame and the sense of unworthiness and the experience of rejection. There can be an end to unreasonable fears and angers. There can be an end to hurting the people we love and driving them away. There can be an end to doing things that cause others to react to us in the ways we most do not want. There can be an end to inner turmoil. There can be peace. That is the good news, or at least some of the consequences of it, that we need to "believe."

What You Believe Is What You Get

Now "believe" means "trust." What you "believe" in is what you put your trust in. Jesus' ministry was telling us about and illustrating for us the good news, which is what the word "gospel" means, which He came to proclaim. To obtain the benefits of which He speaks, we need to put our trust in what He says, what He has done, and who He is. Somewhat similarly, in some measure at least, to derive benefit from the things I note here, which I see as parts of Jesus' good news, you must put some trust in them, at least enough to honestly try them.

Now, while all of the aforesaid is true, the principle of repentance is far less complicated than that may have made it sound. The primary point of the few paragraphs is to point out that in repentance you are *not* giving up what gives your life meaning but what has only *seemed* to be meaningful and has not really worked; and you are not giving up what you know for nothing, but giving up something for something very real and far better; and that was and is and has been God's intent at all times.

Practical Repentance

Repent means you own up to the bad stuff you have done, especially anything related to the incident you are working through at the moment, acknowledging that it is indeed bad, rejecting it in spirit, declaring your rejection of it, and committing yourself to not do it again to the best of your ability. As new wrongful actions come to mind, in addition to those specifically related to the causal event you are working on, you should also ask God to forgive you for those as well. The purpose of this is to receive and to know that you have received God's forgiveness. And you might also ask God's help to keep the new commitments you make as you go. You may very well need some extra help. In case the matter is unclear to you, "bad stuff" is whatever God has said is bad. That is what you need to repent of.

The Reality of Grace

Perhaps you have heard the words from Isaiah 55:8-9: "'My thoughts are not your thoughts, neither are your ways my ways,'" declares the Lord. 'As the heavens are higher than the earth, so are my ways higher than your ways and my thoughts than your thoughts.'" Often I think they are spoken in a manner implying the great unworthiness of man, but that is simply not what God is saying here, as reading them in context will easily show.

Here is what is said in verses 6-7, just before the words cited above: "Seek the Lord while he may be found; call on him while he is near. Let the wicked forsake his way and the evil man his thoughts. Let him turn to the Lord, and he will have mercy on him, and to our God, for he will freely pardon."

The way in which God is different from us is in his mercy! We might very well be inclined to be unforgiving, but that is not God. That is what Isaiah is saying here. I bring this to you because again and again I find that people have difficulty dealing with reality for fear that they will be ultimately condemned, and that is not so – not unless you continue to refuse to deal with reality and acknowledge the truth of God. God wants to give you grace. You can change course; you do have to put your trust in the good news.

The prophet Ezekiel wrote about 570 B. C. In his time, God's people blamed their sufferings upon the sins of their fathers. They used a proverb to express that sentiment: "The fathers have eaten sour grapes, but the children's teeth are set on edge." Ezekiel writes in opposition to that idea, and chapter 18 is where he does so most explicitly. If a father does wrong, but the son turns from the father's wrong and does right, he will not be punished for the sins of the father. Indeed, if a man who has done wrong, turns from the wrong he has done to do right, then he too will escape punishment but now enter into the reward of the righteousness he now does. Again, my point is that the one seeking to do right never needs to fear repentance. Repentance is a means to blessing, not to condemnation.

In Acts 2, the coming of the Holy Spirit on the day of Pentecost is described. The crowds seeing the commotion begin to make jokes about these wild people, and Peter takes that as an opportunity to declare what is going on. After talking about who Jesus was and his resurrection, he declares that what they are seeing is the fulfillment long before prophesied in Joel. Many are struck by what Peter says and ask what they should do. His answer is recorded in Acts 2:38. Please note two things that he says people can receive when they repent, forgiveness and the gift of the Holy Spirit: "Peter replied, 'Repent and be baptized, every one of you, in the name of Jesus Christ for the forgiveness of your sins. And you will receive the gift of the Holy Spirit." Again, my point is that the freedom of forgiveness is possible and additionally we may also receive the indwelling presence of the Holy Sprit of God.

One day Peter and John were going to the Temple to pray. They encounter a lame beggar on the way in. Peter heals him, he begins to walk and leap and praise God, a crowd gathers around in astonishment, and Peter again starts to explain what has happened. He says that he knows they acted in ignorance and did not intend evil, then he tells them what they should do in verse 19: "Repent, then, and turn to God, so that your sins may be wiped out, so that times of refreshing may come from the Lord." That is why I want you to repent of what is not of God: so that times of refreshing may come to you from the Lord.

An Illustration of Repentance

What do you repent of? We need to repent of anything which is not of God. Especially, as we work through a particular incident, we need to explicitly repent of anything which is not of God and which seems to be related to the particular event we are dealing with at the time. For example, if a woman who had been molested, having wrongly concluded that she was not of value, gave herself sexually to many men, she would need to repent of that. If a man who was abused in some manner became a similar sort of abuser, he would need to repent of his abusive conduct. These are merely two possible examples of misconduct done related to misconduct received. We need to try to deal with all that we can think of. (While we may focus on things related to a given event and while God may give us grace to deal with many other things later, any known sin can be a serious hindrance and any willful holding onto a known sin is most exceedingly likely to be a hindrance to healing.)

How do you repent of our sins? You acknowledge that you have done them. You acknowledge that they are not in accord with God's word, and thus that they are wrong. You declare yourself in agreement with God's word and acknowledge that what you did was wrong. You declare your commitment never to do that again, so help you God. And you ask God's help to keep you on the new track you have taken. It might happen much more easily than this. You may not have to put into words each element if your heart has got the right idea.

God Will Help You Do It

Let me share some words of encouragement with you from Paul's letter to the church at Philippi. In 2:12-13, he said, "Therefore, my dear friends, as you have always obeyed – not only in my presence, but now much more in my absence – continue to work out your salvation with fear and trembling, for it is God who works in you to will and to act according to his good purpose." Paul was writing a gracious letter to a church he was well pleased with. So note that this word implies that even good and saved people still have work to do to "work out your salvation." But now the real reasons I showed this passage to you are two. In verse 13, it says that God works in you "to will." God will help you change even your will, your thought patterns, your orientation, your ideation. Do not expect merely to change external conduct and yet be tormented with foul thoughts. You may have to struggle through such a place for a season, but that is not your final destination. You are also to change your very will, and God will be with you in that work. Then Paul says God is also with you "to act according to his good purpose." God will be with you to do the right thing. You will not be alone in this struggle. God will help you.

Finally, while we are in Philippians, let me call your attention to chapter 1, verse 6: I am "confident of this, that he who began a good work in you will carry it on to completion until the day of Jesus Christ." Then too recall Paul's words in Philippians 4:13: "I can do everything through him [Jesus] who gives me strength." The struggle may be difficult at times, it may take more than a moment for some matters, but know that God can get you through. It may be hard, but the new freedom you will find will be well worth it.

Repentance Does Not Focus on Remorse

Repentance does not focus on feeling bad. You may feel remorse. That is entirely appropriate, but that is not the main point. The main point is to change course: to see the error, to reject it, and to strive all you can to do right.

Repentance May or May Not Include Making Amends

Making amends may or may not be necessary. If there is something that you can do in that regard, that would be excellent. Surely, if you now sense that something you did was wrong, you accept responsibility for it, and, having accepted responsibility, you may want to do what you can to "make it right," or make amends. Many things we deal with in this set of spiritual exercises are not readily subject to making amends. You may be repenting of behavior long ago, with people no longer known, or even of behavior discontinued but not quite repented of previously. Making amends may be helpful, but I see it as a secondary issue here. The primary one is to change your course from here on.

Regarding Truth and Grace: Truth

Allow me some small discussion of "truth and grace." In John 1:14, John says: "The Word became flesh and made his dwelling among us. We have seen his glory, the glory of the One and Only, who came from the Father, full of grace and truth." The declaration of this passage is that Jesus was perfectly possessed of both grace and truth. An implication of this passage is that we need to pursue and offer both grace and truth. A further implication is that there *is* such a thing as truth.

I suspect that the secular psychologist will have been pleased enough with the idea of mourning; after all, it is much like the "grief process" spoken of so much in his field. I think he may well be pleased with the notion of forgiveness. When he gets to it he may find much to affirm in "renewing the mind," although that may sound scary to him just now. But I suspect that the secular psychologist may have more trouble with repentance. To call one to repent implies that there is a right and a wrong. There is. Furthermore, everyone, hear that again, *everyone* believes there is right and wrong. However, much contemporary thought, affecting but not limited to psychology, is much afflicted with a relativism that hinders moral choices. It declares that there is no right and wrong, or that all right and wrong are merely human constructs, with no more validity than what individuals choose to give to them. I believe that is clearly and seriously mistaken.

It is the Christian position that man, which means male and female, is made in the image of God. There are things which are in conformity with that image and things which are not. To live a life *not* in conformity with that image is like trying to put a round peg in a square hole. It does not fit, and the abrasion one feels is the natural and inevitable result of this mismatch. If that is so, then declaring something healthy does not make it so. If there is some sort of objective standard, even if imperfectly known or understood, then rejecting that standard will not make it any less true than declaring that gravity is false and trying to jump off a high building in the expectation that you can defy it. That is why repentance is necessary. That is why it is helpful. And it has been proven to be so not only in my limited work, but in the lives of persons and nations across the millennia.

I suspect that the "secular" or non-Christian attempt to use "repentance" must call upon the troubled person to "repent" of what is not in accord with *their own* beliefs. I also suspect that, unless their beliefs be in accord with the mind of God, that will not work. It will require an ever expanding circle of redefinitions of language and readjustment of expectations to try to make a false system seem sound. It will make the Ptolemaic solar system look a model of simplicity. You are, however, welcome to try. I hope your frustration leads you to consider the claims of Christ.

Regarding Truth and Grace: Grace

Some among the Christian tribe may have trouble with the other part of that declaration in John 1:14, "grace." I would submit that there is no true truth without grace, just as there is no true grace without truth. Does it arise from a fear that our hold on truth is so feeble? Does it arise from a fear that others might find us too weakly orthodox if we do not berate the errant soul quickly and firmly enough? Does it arise from a lack of grace? A lack of grace received? And thus too weak an ability to give it? I do not know, but I find we humans are sometimes odd mixes and I suspect multiple causality is the case. Still, the concern remains: We must uphold grace as well as truth.

The people of false grace, who lie about truth in the name of grace, do not make grace any easier. Every note of grace is at risk of being taken for acceptance of evil. To ward off that risk, some may thump on truth when it might have been better to say nothing, or some may imply acceptance of evil in speaking acceptance of the person in the presence of expected rejection. To uphold both truth and grace is not easy, but the difficulty of the task does not diminish its need.

Ephesians 4:13, does not say, literally, that we "should speak the truth in love." It says, literally, we "should truth in love." Oh, I suppose the meaning is much the same, but it brings out still more clearly the element of love. If someone has come to you to share their deepest thoughts, fears and embarrassments, it is most likely that they, and every bit of their story, should be treated with the utmost respect and care.

There is absolutely no question that each of us needs to repent of wrongdoing. There is a true truth, and God is it. But grace is also essential; no, not merely necessary, but even essential. Grace is of the essence of God. It not only goes far to make possible the repentance, it is a part of the truth. It is a part of what we repent to, and what we repent in. Bear that in mind too.

Chapter Nine:
Re-Program Your Understanding

*Do not conform any longer to the pattern of this world,
but be transformed by the renewing of your mind.
Then you will be able to test and approve what God's will
is his good, pleasing and perfect will.*
– *Romans 12:2*

Physically, I suppose, some medical examinations and some acts of molestation may be very similar, but emotionally, psychologically and spiritually they are radically different. Why? What makes them different?

It is the meaning that each event has. In the molestation event, even a mild one which *might* not be *physically* much more intrusive than some medical examinations, the person is bemeaned. The person's worth is set at nothing. The person's will is violated. The person's dignity is shoved aside. The person is coerced into conduct that can only be obtained through force or threat of force, and any such event then also threatens the person's very life.

In events of molestation, physical abuse, severe illness and such, the person may come to feel that he or she is not of worth. They must not be of worth, they reason, for such a thing to have happened to them. The person may conclude that he/she is not loved by God. After all, they reason, God could not care about them if He let this happen. The person may conclude that they can never trust men or women or people, since a man or a woman or some person did this to them. A molested woman may conclude that it is not safe to be a woman, and may try to make herself more of a man. A molested man may conclude that it is not good to be a man, and he may reject his masculinity since he associates it with the evil done to him. And these are only a few of the trajectories of reason, reasonable but untrue, which the mind of the abused person may follow. Usually, mind you, all of this is *not* consciously done. These are real reactions, real "decisions" you might say, but not, usually, conscious ones. After all, they are often made when a person is but a child and has very little language or understanding by means of which to make these decisions consciously.

How We Make "Unconscious" Decisions

I speak again of an incident I mentioned before, but I will tell you other things, and I have a different point to make. In 1968, I lived in Venice, California. My father had just died, and I had just returned from my parents' home in Temple City, to Venice. It was my first morning back. I was out walking and jogging a bit. I was about to cross a street near my home. I looked north, and I saw a bus stopped there. I assumed that it was stopped because the light required it to be stopped, and therefore all traffic from that direction would be stopped. I looked south as I went into the street. Traffic there was quite far enough away for me to cross safely. But what I did not realize was that the bus was not stopped for the light but to let passengers on or off, and that there was a car coming at full speed on the other side of the bus. Very shortly after I entered the street, I heard something, I saw something out of the corner of my left eye, and I was hit by a car. I think it is probably fortunate that it was a Volkswagen. It was small, and it had a rounded front end that probably made it easier for me to roll into it, rather than be run over by it. I was hit on the left side, I flew over the car, smashing its windshield with my head, and I landed in the pavement in my right side. I was taken to the emergency room at UCLA Hospital.

Setting aside various interesting but irrelevant details, after a time I was to be released to go home. I called my mother to come and pick me up. Aside from various scrapes and bruises, I had a very swollen right hip (the unresolved hematoma I spoke of before), where I had landed. I would not be driving for a few days at least. Consequently, whenever I went anywhere for the next week or so, my mother drove. Whenever we got anywhere close to another car, not dangerously close, not improperly close, just close, I got a knot in my stomach. I did not "decide" to get a knot in my stomach. I just did. I could tell myself that we were not really that close, but that did no good at all – at least for a season. I felt sick to my stomach. I was in fear for my life. I did not "decide" to be in fear, not consciously, I just was. Fortunately for me, I was an adult when this happened (twenty-two), and I could reason out the problem, and it diminished after a few days or so and left me after a couple of weeks or so.

What I am describing is a post-traumatic stress

disorder. It happens, it automatically happens, when any life-threatening event, or seemingly life-threatening event, takes place. This automatic response is probably a part of our built-in survival mechanism. It can be very helpful in some situations. It can be harmful in others. I remember stories of co-workers who came back from Vietnam who would dive for cover at a loud bang. That was very helpful in the boonies in Vietnam; that was less helpful back home when a car going by backfired.

This is essentially what we are dealing with in the "healing of memories." The wounded spirit has made internalized adjustments to survive. Certain actions threaten one's life, and one must take action to avoid the threat. New events seem to threaten the same thing, and we dive for cover at the sound of a harmless backfire. But in the matters with which we deal here, our response may be to refuse to trust anyone, with a consequent inability to have a real relationship with anyone. Or our response may be to get aggressive, we think (subconsciously) to protect ourselves, but find ourselves continually creating conflict. Or we hide from all manner of social interactions, we think (subconsciously) to protect ourselves from further harm, but we end up in snuffing out our very life.

Another Illustration

I worked in East L. A. for fourteen years. Where I worked was a great place in many ways, but it was not a Sunday School picnic. One guy had a steal-to-order business [You put in your order, and he had it stolen for you!], another sold clothes from his wife's place of work at a very steep discount, another guy ran the horse book, another had the football cards, another dealt pot, another dealt pills, a couple loan sharked, some were coyotes, at least one did some part-time pimping, and various ones slept with a shotgun by their bed or carried a rifle from their apartment to their car every day for safety's sake. I worked a lot of the graveyard shift for a season, from about 10:00 p.m. to 5:30 a.m., more or less. We had been talking about a lot of dangerous incidents one night. After work, I went home. It was still dark. As I was walking along my walkway, I saw a car pull slowing into the driveway of the apartment building alongside mine. Why was he going so slowly? Then I saw some round, cylindrical object sticking out of the window. I could not see very well. What was it? Was it a gun? Was someone going to take a shot at me? That was the kind of thing we had just been talking about. There was a small concrete block wall, no more than three-feet high, between my property and the adjoining one. I was just about to dive into the dirt alongside the wall when my eyes could focus clearly enough to see that the round, cylindrical object sticking out of the car window was the newspaper. He was coming to deliver the morning paper. We do not respond to what *is*, but to what we *think* is.

We Respond to What We *Think* Is

One of my favorite illustrations comes from one of the books by Father John Powell. I may change the specifics a little, but the point will be clear. A man had just bought a new home in one of the new developments somewhere. Make the place wherever you are, Pasadena, New Rochelle, Clairemont, North Las Vegas, Marietta, whatever. They had some services in, but they did not have much in the way of street lights yet, and it was already dark. It had been a long day, and he was eager to get inside and kick back. He got out of his car and he began to head for his door, but then he stopped short. There in his front yard was a huge snake. He backed up against his car. Then he recalled that he had left a hoe over against the side of the garage. He went and got that. Very carefully, he came back to where he had seen the snake. It was still there. Then he began to hack at it with his hoe. The snake jumped and writhed as he hacked away at it with his hoe. Finally, he stopped, and when he paused, he saw that the snake did not move any more either. He decided that it was dead. He carefully went around it and got inside his house. It took him a while to calm down after that, but eventually, he got to sleep. He felt much better in the morning. He went to his front door to look at the snake in his yard. He opened his front door, and there, in his front yard was his garden hose, all hacked to pieces.

It was only a garden hose. It had been only a garden hose all along. There was no snake. But his breathing had been labored. His pulse raced. His blood pressure increased. He got sweaty. Adrenalin was pumped into his bloodstream. He believed that he was in a fight for his life. We do *not* respond to what *is*. We respond to what we *think* is. If what we think is wrong, our responses will be off.

Once Again: Belief Shapes Life

Here is a story you know. It is by Hans Christian Anderson, more or less. Consider it again. There was this awkward little duck. He was the least attractive duck of all. In fact he was known as the ugly duckling. Mother barely paid attention to him. The other little ducklings all shunned him at school. He had to eat his lunch alone, and at recess, he had to play by himself. He could not swim like the other ducklings. He did not look like the other ducklings. He felt like a total retard. He felt very sad and dejected. He knew that he was worthless.

From time to time, he would see some magnificent birds fly over head and he wished ever so much that he might be like one of them. Then he would be big and beautiful and he could just fly away from all these ducks that did not like him. One day, he saw one of these big beautiful birds, they were called swans, land at a pond nearby. He thought he would go over and just look at him. After all, he had nothing better to do. He was pleased to see this beautiful bird, even if he would never be beautiful like that. He looked at the sawn, then he looked at the swan's refection in the pond, then he saw his own reflection in the pond, then he looked back and forth again. What was this? That was him! He was not an ugly duckling! He was not any sort of duck at all. He was a swan, a big beautiful swan! Now he knew who he really was, and that was wonderful.

We Do Not Respond to What Is, But To What We Think Is! And If Our Thinking Is Off, So Will Our Lives Be.

We do not respond to what *is*. We respond to what we *think is*. If what we think is wrong, we will have grief. If we think we are an ugly duckling, we may go through life in misery and dejection. Feeling worthless, we will act in ways that produce and reproduce the very acts of rejection that we cannot stand! Our actions will tend to bring about reactions in others confirming all the lies we hope are false, we feel must be false, and yet fear are true.

The evil one uses lies, often based upon the very real and very bad things that have happened to us, to tell us we are ugly ducks, or that we are under attack from snakes when it is only a garden hose, or that someone is about to shoot at us when they are just delivering the morning paper.

We Need to Correct Our Wrong Beliefs

We need to repent of wrong beliefs and allow Christ to renew our minds in the truths of God. God does love us. We are made in his image, and that is very, very good. We can trust God, and man and woman and others. If we are a man, it is a great thing to be a man; it is a part of God's perfect plan for us; and it is very fulfilling, honorable and good. If we are a woman, it is a great thing to be a woman; it is a part of God's perfect plan for us; and it is very fulfilling, honorable and good. We are *not* condemned to live our lives for ever in fear, nor torn by anger, nor captured by immorality. All these things are lies of the enemy, and we are to recognize that, declare that, discover God's truth, proclaim God's truth, and allow

God to renew our minds in his truth, thereby transforming our very spirits.

Your Experience of Your Earthly Father Powerfully Shapes Your Understanding of Your Heavenly Father

The cancer did not kill her. In fact the autopsy showed that the cancer was gone. It was the medicine they gave her to kill the cancer that made her subject to the rare disease that did kill her, but let's back up a little. It was one of the first times that I noticed a correlation between an ancient injury and a recent illness. A woman came to me who had cancer. Although it was internal, it was focused in a region of the lower back. Sometime along the way, I discovered that her father had often beat her, and one time he beat her severely, almost to death, and primarily it was focused in this area of her lower back.

There were many hurts across the years, and there was much healing. A sister who lived more than a hundred miles away began to come to church, at least for a while, because she recognized something had changed in her sister. The woman herself said that she would have been dead years earlier if some of the healing in the spirit that happened for her had not, and I believe her. But there is just one thing I want to speak of: She had believed that her father hated her. She came to know that he was a troubled man, but he really and truly loved her.

Many people have a hard time believing in the love of God the Father, if they have not experienced love from the earthly fathers. In fact, you tell me truly about a person's relationship with his earthly father as he was growing up, and, unless there has been some specific reason for change, I will tell what his or her relationship with their heavenly Father is. You will usually find that their true beliefs about God will reflect quite well what they felt in their relationship with their earthly father. (You may occasionally have to look past some theological mutterings - that they do not really believe but say because they think they ought to believe them - in order to find out what they really believe at an emotional level, but when you do, you will usually find what I have just noted.)

This woman had also believed that God the Father was mean, vindictive and wanted to harm her. She loved Jesus, but feared and tended to hate "God." Christians should readily recognize the irony here. We say that God is one. So how can this be? By the way, it is fairly common! Many Christians have only the fuzziest notion of the Trinity, and many people, Christians included, have a "gut level" aversion to God since they associate Him with the rejection or abuse they felt they received from their earthly fathers. She had felt profoundly rejected by her earthly father and thus she hated her heavenly Father.

In this woman's case, there was more grief added to her understanding of God the Father. She had been left, at far too young an age (about seven, as I recall), to care for two or more other, younger children. This was long ago. They were left in a small home, a cabin really, in winter with a wood burning stove for heat. The girls were playing; a younger girl opened the door to the stove and got herself on fire. The older child, all of seven, got her outside in the snow and tried to put out the fire, but she could not do so in time. The younger girl died. She felt responsible. She was told that she was responsible by comments made by adults who were trying to ease their own guilt and pain. And right after that, the preacher at her church gave a hellfire and damnation message. From this message, after his horrific event, at seven years old, she got the impression that God would send this poor little girl to hell and probably her too. That was another reason she did not like "God" even though she loved Jesus.

After we worked through her pain in the manner I outline here, she came to know that God loved her too, and she loved Him. But for many decades she carried this great conflict with God around with her. Part of the healing in her relationship with God the Father came from the healing in her relationship with her earthly father, something which was achieved long after he had died.

Replant the Garden of Your Mind

In earlier versions of this teaching, I would call this part two of repenting. The first part was repenting of wrong actions, and this part was repenting of wrong beliefs. It is still that, or rather it still requires that, but repenting of wrong beliefs alone is insufficient. It is something like cutting off the tops of weeds and being surprised that they grow back.

Forty odd years ago, there was a story in *Time* magazine about a con man in India. He went to different villages. He told people that if they did what he told them, they could turn lead into gold. He put lead into a pot, he stirred, and after a while he pulled out gold. People were very impressed. For a fee, he told them that he would tell them how they could do the same thing. They paid him the fee. Then just before they began to do the important stirring, he told them there was one thing to be aware of. Whatever they did, they must not think about monkeys. If they thought about monkeys, it would not work. And low and behold, they all thought about monkeys, and that was why it did not work, and that was why he did not have to give them back their fees - at least until people got wise to him.

If you focus on what you must not do, you are almost sure to do it. You do not need merely to cut off the tops of weeds; you need to pull them out. Indeed, since there are always more weed spores floating around in the air, even that alone will not work. In order to be weed free, you must not only pull out the weeds, but you must also plant flowers. With established flowers, the weeds will have a hard time getting established, even if a few spores blow your way. That is why we need not only to repent, but also to be renewed. You need to re-program your understanding.

Paul says, "Do not conform any longer to the pattern of this world." This implies that some of the world's patterns do not work or are not wise. Does that make sense? It should. Anyone can see that there are many messes in our world, so something must be messed up. Furthermore, we are speaking of specific situations where an individual has found that something in his or her life is not working well. That must mean that some pattern they have conformed to is not working, is not right. There is some pattern or belief or action or reaction to which he or she should no longer conform.

Then Paul goes on to say, "But be transformed." In Greek, there are two words that speak of form. The word used here for "transformed" speaks not just of a different form, or version of the same basic form, but of a new form in kind. Paul is saying, "Get a new basic structure." He is speaking of genuine transformation.

Perhaps the most critical phrase for us comes next: "By the renewing of your mind." Here he is telling us how this basic restructuring is to be accomplished. Your very mind is to be changed, made new, or renewed. Your understanding needs to change. Now this is true of many people in many ways, but I am focusing here on the change of understanding that needs to take place with regards to the wrong beliefs imbibed by one's spirit as a result of injuries to the spirit.

Thus, for example, if a molested person has concluded that he or she is of no value, that is in conflict with the word of God that he or she has been made in the image of God, as noted in Genesis 1:27, and thus is wrong. If they have believed that they were not of worth, they need to "repent" of that mistaken belief. Declare the righteousness of God's truth and ask God to secure them in this new understanding.

If, for example, a molested male or female has concluded that it was not good for them to be male or female, as the case may be, that too conflicts with the word of God, as noted in Genesis 1:27, and thus is also wrong. If they find that they have believed that, they need to acknowledge that they have, acknowledge that they were wrong to do so, and ask God to confirm them in their new and right understanding of the virtue and value of being male or female.

A person brought up in a home filled with anger, might have concluded that there is no security in his or her life. That conclusion conflicts with Psalm 27:10, Proverbs 3:5, and John 14:1, among other verses, and therefore it is wrong. If they discover that they have believed that, they need to acknowledge that, repent of that, declare what is true, and ask God to confirm that truth within them.

A person brought up in an alcoholic home might, for example, have concluded that he or she is responsible to make everything in a dysfunctional system work. Romans 12:18 indicates that it is not always possible to make all things come out right and that you are responsible to do what you can, but not to make all things right. Ezekiel 18 indicates that each is responsible for his or her own conduct. If you recognize that you have taken on a responsibility which is not yours, according to God's word, then again you need to repent, proclaim truth, and seek to secure yourself in that new truth.

These are all only illustrations of possible misconceptions to which foul experiences in life may have helped to lead a person. We are responsible for our own thoughts. (See Matthew 5:21-48 again if need be.) Thus, once we recognize our error we need to do all we can to correct our understanding. We do that by checking with God's word. It is the standard. We acknowledged the truth as we come to understand it. We repent of our errors as we see them, and we proclaim the truth. Then we ask God to confirm our new understandings. We ask God to re-program our understanding in the light of his truths.

Paul goes on to say that when we have allowed our minds to be transformed by conformity to the will of God, then we will be able to verify that God's way is right. "Then you will be to test and approve what God's will is – his good, pleasing and perfect will." There are many who reject God's ways who have never tried them and know nothing of them.

One time I invited a young man to brunch at the Huntington Sheraton. There were more than a dozen salads, numerous vegetable dishes, a dozen different entrees, and another dozen or more desserts, but he would have nothing but a cheeseburger. You do not get what you will not try. To paraphrase C. S Lewis, it is not that people have tried God's ways and found them wanting; they have found them difficult and left them untried. Paul tells us here in Romans 12:2, that when we try it we will like it. We will find that his way is good, pleasing and perfect.

From Victim to Victor

There is much that we can do simply by seeing the truth and acknowledging it. And simply once seeing the truth can be life changing. However, thinking new thoughts is not always quick or easy. We may be helped by trustworthy brothers or sisters reminding us of the encouraging truth we need to know. Generally speaking, reminding us of error is *not* very helpful, for that tends to confirm our condemnation. This is true especially if we have already acknowledged the error and made a commitment to leave it behind. Reminding us of the real truth in a way that encourages us to be fully who God intends us to be, can be. Sometimes we may wish to begin making lists of Bible verses that affirm the things we need to believe in ways we are able to receive them. We may review them from time to time. Or we may simply note new confirming verses as we find them in our ongoing devotional readings. We may also go back to specific passages which we have found spoke powerful encouragement to us at one time.

Fundamentally, renewing the mind is begun by …
1. Seeing right belief,
2. Specifically renouncing wrong belief we have discovered,
3. Affirming right belief,
4. And asking God to secure us in the right belief.

The result of this work is that the victim can become a victor. Both the victim and the victor have endured some difficult experience. But one is broken by it and still held captive by it. The other has overcome it. Yes, he or she was attacked; yes, it hurt; yes, there was damage and loss; but, no, he or she is not destroyed by it, their soul is not warped by it. It was, perhaps, but is no more.

JIM HILL

Chapter Ten: You've Got to Ask

When he came down from the mountainside, large crowds followed him. A man with leprosy came and knelt before him and said, "Lord, if you are willing, you can make me clean." Jesus reached out his hand and touched the man. "I am willing," he said. "Be clean!" Immediately he was cured of his leprosy." – Matthew 8:1-3

I have used this passage in Matthew 8 about Jesus healing a leper for a reason. It illustrates Jesus willingness to heal. Lepers were the most despised unfortunates of their day. Recall the days a few years ago when AIDS was not only incurable but virtually untreatable and a short-term death sentence. Many people shunned AIDS sufferers, fearing for their own safety and, often, acting out scorn for the AIDS sufferers' perceived sins. Lepers were treated worse. It too was incurable in antiquity. It was also more contagious than AIDS is. The only protection for those not infected was to "quarantine" all those who were, for ever. But this meant for the leper never again to be a part of society. Even his family was obliged to shun the leper since they could otherwise be carriers. Family members might leave food somewhere for them, but not have contact with them. Their lot was never again to touch or be touched, never again to have any sort of social life, except possibly with some other lepers. Lepers were supposed to stay away from others and to call out, "Unclean" if any came near, for the protection of the uninfected. One rabbi was proud of his habit of throwing rocks at lepers to keep them away from people. Lepers were outcasts and something of a universal whipping boy.

For Jesus to touch this man was to break the law! Jesus broke the law to heal this man. If need be, Jesus will break the rules to heal you too. We need to trust that. Somehow we need to ask for healing. Perhaps it is that if we have not asked, then we have not yet dared to hope, and that lack of daring, that lack of trust, that lack of faith, will keep us from getting the healing that is available to us.

There was a ritual given in Leviticus for restoration when one had been healed of leprosy, but it had never been used. No Israelite had ever been healed of leprosy.

In the whole of human history known to them, no one had ever been healed. (Naaman was healed, but he was a foreigner and thus not subject to Levitical ritual.) It took great faith for this utter outcast to come to Jesus and to believe that he could heal him. You may need to have faith of similar strength. The ones who did not come, did not get healed. Those who came and those who asked, did.

Healing Is a Major Part of the Gospel

There are over a hundred references to healing in the gospels, some references are to individuals and others are to great crowds, with a few dozen more such references in the rest of the New Testament. Twice in Mathew's gospel, at 4:23 and at 9:35, Jesus' ministry is described as three-fold: Teaching, preaching and healing. This indicates that Jesus could heal, and that healing people mattered to Him.

There are instances of healing recorded by in the early church by Peter, Paul and Philip. And the letter of James implies that it was and is normative for there to be prayer for healing in the church. This indicates that healing was not *only* for Jesus to do.

Hebrews 13:8 says "Jesus Christ is the same yesterday today and forever." This indicates that what Jesus did during his earthly ministry, He is able to do now.

There Is Authority in Jesus' Name

Peter in Acts 3:16 makes is quite clear that whatever healing "we" "do" is actually done "in the name of Jesus Christ." "In the name of" someone means "in the character and authority" of the person named.

There are spiritual realities. And we who are in Christ have authority to act in his name. In Matthew 28, in verses 18-20, Jesus is quotes as saying, "All authority in heaven and earth has been given to me. Therefore go and make disciples of all nations, baptizing them in the name of the Father and of the Son and of the Holy Spirit, and teaching them to obey everything I have commanded you. And surely I am with you always, to the very end of the age." Several things are said here, but one thing I want to note is that the directive to his followers to go and do was predicated upon the fact that all authority was given to him in heaven and on earth. The implication is that we can now do what He asks us to do *because* He has all this authority, and thus it is further implied that we can act *in his authority*. That understanding is confirmed by his subsequent statement that He will be "with us" always, even to the end of the age, presumably to support our fulfillment of his command by his presence. For further support for this idea, consider also Matthew 10:8 and Luke 10:1-18. Jesus desires to heal, Jesus has authority to heal, and we have authority to call upon his authority and even to act in it.

If you saw Sergeant Preston of the Yukon on TV back in the fifties, you may recall him telling someone to "open in the name of the crown." By those words he declared that he came in the authority of all the government of Canada and, indeed, of the entire British Empire. You were commanded to open not to Tom, Dick or Harry, but to "the crown." In American police TV shows and movies of the forties and fifties, you might very well hear a policeman say, "Open in the name of the law." He too was saying that he did not come in his own authority, but that he demanded compliance in response to all the authority which the government had granted to him.

William Barclay, in one of his commentaries, tells a story about a riot in India sometime in the nineteenth century. A merchant, I believe it was, not even a government official, fearing for his safety and knowing the authority that Britain had there at the time, put some piece of paper with some British governmental seal on it at the gate to his compound. This was sufficient to make all the rioters pass him by, leaving him entirely unharmed.

In 2006, there was a story about Art Shell being the coach of the Raiders again. The very able and very famous and very well paid Randy Moss committed a false start penalty in practice, and Art made him run laps. He may not have had the physical power to force him to run laps, but he had the authority to make him do it.

What we do, we do in Jesus' name, that is, in his authority. And we have great authority when we act in his name, in his character and authority. One time, desiring to weaken a certain unclean spirit's hold on a person, I asked the spirit if there were angels in the room. The spirit, using the person's body, opened her eyes and began to look. As it/she swept the room, her eyes got wider and wider as it/she saw more and more angels. It confirmed with awe that there were indeed many angels in the room, and that was a sign of the presence and power of God. I cite this incident only to illustrate that we do have authority in Jesus' name.

Recall that I always pray God's presence into the room and upon each of us as we begin to do this work. Recall also that I usually ask the Holy Spirit to reveal to the person what we need to work with. Then, at times of hesitation or blockage in the process, I will freely ask the Father to let his Holy Spirit lead, direct or bring to mind, as need be, praying in the name of Jesus. Recall also that as each step of the pattern is worked out, I ask the person coming for help to pray through each step, telling God what they need to say. When they mourn, they tell God how wrong it was, how much it hurt, how much damage it has done, and perhaps how much it still hurts. When they forgive, I ask them to tell God that they forgive the specific person or persons they need to forgive and for what specific injuries they forgive them. When they repent, I ask them to tell God of their newly recognized error, their sorrow at that error, their rejection of wrong conduct, their commitment to do right, and their request that God help them keep their commitments. When they seek to renew their mind or understanding, again they tell God of their sorrow over wrong belief, they declare right belief, and they ask God's help to secure them in right belief. When they ask God to heal, they may or may not repeat some of the things just noted, but now they will ask specifically for the healing of the presenting problems, the problems they were aware of when they came, and any other problems they may have uncovered in the course of the prayer time. Everything is done with prayer in Jesus' name.

One way that this is a work of God is that I continually ask his presence, guidance and power in all that we do. Another way that this is a work of God is that we are applying principles which I believe are godly, biblical principles. These are principles that God has used in the construction of the world and that God has revealed to us in his word, the Bible. The principles upon which this work rests are noted in brief below:

1. Effects have causes.

2. There is a divine order, and our pain may indicate that we are out of it.

3. We need to deal with reality, or face facts.

4. We should get God involved, by asking Jesus Christ to be Lord and Savior, and by asking the guidance of the Holy Spirit.

5. Mourn. Tell God how wrong it was and how much it hurt.

6. Forgive the perpetrator. Surrender vengeance to God.

7. Repent of any wrong conduct of yours, especially any related in any way to the event which you are working through.

8. Re-program your understanding. Renew or transform your mind. Discover the wrong beliefs your spirit has imbibed because of the perceived trauma it received, discover the truth, renounce the wrong beliefs, work to secure yourself in right belief, and ask God to secure you in right belief.

9. Specifically ask Jesus to heal you of the original problems and any others you now think you need to present to Him.

Ask and Receive

At one time, I had thought to call this section "Receive." Then I could have had three sections in a row beginning with "R": Repent, Renew and Receive. Alliteration always makes things easier to remember and that is a benefit. And we do need to be able to receive the healing which God desires to give. This could be a very helpful word for some: Allow yourself to receive what God wants to give you. However, "receive" is passive, and I thought that was too great a drawback. "You've got to ask" Jesus to heal is not flashy, cute or clever, but it obliges us to recognize that we must want something from God and we must do something to obtain it. We do have to ask.

"Ask and it will be given to you; seek and you will find; knock and the door will be opened to you. For everyone who asks receives; he who seeks finds; and to him who knocks, the door will be opened." – Matthew 7:7-8.

JIM HILL

Chapter Eleven: God Did Not Abandon You

And surely I am with you always, to the very end of the age. – Matthew 28:20
If I go up to the heavens, you are there; if I make my bed in the depths, you are there.
– Psalm 138:8

Theologically, the Christian "knows" that God is omnipresent, that means that He is at all places at all times. But we really cannot make any sense out of that since it is totally beyond our frame of reference. Since that is so, however little we really grasp that idea, that should mean that God was with us also in our times of deepest hurt, abuse or abandonment. If that were so, as our theology would tell us it should be, then that might provide comfort. But frankly, it does not provide much comfort, since it is all just words to us, usually. Indeed, it might make the injury even more painful if we were to believe that God was there and yet He still allowed the terrible things that happened to us to happen. What follows did not arise from my theology, but from my stumbling forward as I felt God guide me. It did, however, confirm such theology. And it is very real and it has been very helpful.

Remember that I do not do "imagery exercises." Others do, and I cast no aspersions on that practice. It may enable them to work with people with whom I cannot, or it may enable individuals to work more easily with groups of people at the same time, or it may save time even in working with one person. But I do not do it. I do not tell people what to see. I ask them what they do see. I may ask God to tell them what they need to see, but I do not tell them what to see. I do not pick the incidents or issues for them. I ask them to tell me what they think we should work on, and if they are stuck, I ask God to tell them, and then they can tell me.

When we struggle to recall the specific events of a given incident, I work very hard to avoid planting any thoughts or ideas. I ask open ended questions. If I feel I must ask a question about a specific possibility, I will give two or three or more possible answers so as not to lead someone to a given answer. I will then speak in as bland a manner as possible so as not to turn a person towards or away from a given answer. I am never shocked or angered or otherwise affected by an answer so as not to cause discomfort in recalling what needs to be recalled.

When they have worked through an issue, I do not ask them to envision taking it to Jesus, or to see themselves go to Jesus. I do not ask them to imagine anything.

However, at some point in my own journey of discovery, having read and heard that people sometimes see things in the spiritual realm, I began to ask people if they saw anything in the spiritual realm. If they said, "Well, I don't see anything, but I can imagine it," I said, "No, that's alright. If it comes, alright; if it doesn't come alright." My rationale is that if they see it and I have not planted it or told them to see it or asked them to imagine it, it will have more impact when they do see something in the spiritual realm. I find that to be so. I offer no complaint about the patterns used by any other. God works in many ways. But I am comfortable with my decision here. I "trade" easier and possibly broader use for greater impact or meaning. Now then, here is some of what I began to discover when I asked people to tell me if they saw anything in the spiritual realm.

"He's Holding Back the Black."

A woman was beaten severely by her father at the age of four, perhaps nearly to death. We went through all the steps outlined above of mourning, forgiving, repenting, renewing the mind and asking Jesus to heal. Then I asked her to look again at the scene. I asked her to describe it a little so that I knew she had something specific in mind. Then I asked her to tell me if she could see anything in the spiritual realm.

At first she could not. I asked her to look again. "Oh, she said, "he's in a wall of black." Her father was in a wall of black. Then I asked her if she could see Jesus there. She could not. I asked her to look again. "No. He couldn't be here. It's too horrible. (pause) Oh, He's holding back the black." I do not know if Jesus' holding back the black meant that He kept her from being killed or if it meant that He kept her from being consumed in the same kind of anger that her father was. But this did tell us three things: 1) God was there, 2) She was not alone, 3) And God did do something specific to help her. It helped to know that God did and does love her and that she was not abandoned. She got physical, emotional and spiritual healing. Over time, she knew *more* about things that had happened to her, not less, including more bad things that she had previously had no memory of, *but they no longer held the pain they had*. She also came to know that her father truly loved her, contrary to what she had believed nearly all her life. She also came to be able to truly forgive him. This also enabled her to draw closer to her heavenly Father.

"These Are Not My Feet."

Another woman dealt with an incident where she was at the home of her husband's family, and her husband's family was continually criticizing her, and her husband, who was there, was not defending her – again. After we had worked through the mourning, forgiveness, repentance, renewing and requested God's healing, I asked her to tell me if she saw anything in the spiritual realm. At first she did not. I asked her to look towards the door. She saw nothing. After a moment, I asked her to look at her feet. Her eyes were closed as she sat in my office. Her head bent down as if she were looking at her feet. Then she said, "These are not my feet." At that point I knew whose feet they were, but I always try not to plant ideas, so I simply asked her, "Whose feet are they?" And her reply was, "They're Jesus' feet." Somehow, she sensed that Jesus was there soaking up the humiliation with her or on her behalf. She was not alone. God did care about her. And that knowledge is healing.

An Angel Led Her Back

Another time, a woman had dealt with an incident where her play friends had, apparently intentionally, ditched her when she was a young child, and now she was lost. After having done the things spoken of above, I asked her to look in the spiritual realm. She discovered that she had truly been lost and that an angel had come and shown her the way back to a street she knew.

Jesus Unlocked the Door

Another time, a woman, at the age of twelve, had been called to her pastor's office. She went happily, but then he tried to molest her. She managed to get to the door and get out. After we did the mourning, forgiving, repenting, renewing and requesting of God's help, I asked her to tell me what she saw in the spiritual realm. After a moment, she said, "Oh, I had forgotten that he had locked the door." What she reported she saw was that Jesus had come and unlocked the door so that she could get out. She now remembered that the pastor had previously locked the door so she could not get out. If you take this report at face value, and, in the absence of a reason not to, I do, then God was there, and He did something in the physical realm to set her free. This too was a sign of God's caring for her.

God Was There for Him

A young man came home from school. He had a friend with him. He was about to go into his house. He opened the door first, and then he saw his mother, lying on the couch, drunk, again. He made up some quick excuse (he had had practice), and he and his friend did not go in. It was another instance of humiliation for him. He came to see God there also.

Jesus and Angels Were There to Help

The man who came for prayer of commiseration before his scheduled surgery, but finally agreed to see if we could find any spiritual cause, found one and no longer needed surgery, had recalled an event when he and his father went fishing. He had caught a fish. His father was caught up in his own concerns and did not acknowledge his sons' accomplishment, and this was, I believe, characteristic of his experience of his father. We worked his memory through the process: Mourn, Forgive, Repent, Renew, and Request God's healing. Then I asked him if he could see anything in the spiritual realm. He too saw Jesus there. He also saw an angel. Jesus was there to comfort him.

Jesus Kept Her from Harm

Another woman came with great insecurity. Having prayed the Holy Spirit to reveal what we needed to work with, God brought to mind an incident many years before when a group of men had accosted her while heading home one night. Eventually, she was able to get away without being harmed as they had threatened.

Again, we mourned, forgave, repented, renewed and requested God's help. Then I asked her if she could see anything in the spiritual realm. She did. Jesus was there.

Rapists Were Confounded

Another time a woman was in a country that had fighting going on. In the turmoil, she stopped to spend the night at a friend's house rather than risk being out for the rest of the trip to her own place. She had been in the habit of taking sleeping pills because she could not easily get to sleep with all the turmoil. Her friend proved not to be much of a friend. He came into her room and raped her. After going through the spiritual exercises we have found helpful (Mourn, Forgive, Repent, Renew, Request God's healing), I asked her to see what she could in the spiritual realm. Yes, she saw the Lord there, and somehow God prevented the perpetrator from completing his act.

This has been reported to me before. There was penetration, but the act was not completed. Another woman was used by a group, an unholy group. The process was gone through, and then, when the time came to see what could be seen in the spiritual realm, she saw many things. She saw evil. And she saw evil frustrated. The perpetrator was not able to complete his act, and she saw that the perpetrator was very angry in his frustration. It gave her comfort to know that the evil man was frustrated in his attempt to plant his seed in her.

Jesus Was There to Comfort

A man, as a young boy, was obliged by his father to wait in the car, right outside the window of the bedroom where his father was having his affair with his mistress. When the time came to see what he might in the spiritual realm, he too saw the Lord there to comfort him.

And More

Of course, I could give you many other instances, but I think these suffice to illustrate the general pattern. Once we have dealt with an injurious incident, I commonly ask people if they want to look to see what they can in the spiritual realm. If they do not want to look, I do not ask the Father to have the Holy Spirit help them see. If they do, then we go ahead. I suppose that we generally retrieve memories when we recall incidents; if it is not that, then it might be a revelation from God. I suppose also that the spirit sees these other things of the spirit, but we are accustomed to not seeing and so they do not register. Assuming that, I suppose that it is a retrieval of memory to see into the spirit realm also. However, it may well be that God grants an ability to see things not seen before in any way. People are also able to see things that they could not see at the time! They can see behind themselves for example. I cannot explain the mechanism; I can only report what happens.

Different people at different times have reported seeing, Jesus, angels, light, demons, and light or darkness around certain people. They have also seen physical things they had not recalled before had happened. Sometimes they also have some knowledge of things going on with the perpetrators. I do not see these things. I have never seen angels or demons or the rest of it. I do not tell people to see these things ahead of time. I do not tell them what things to see. *I do not ask them to see; I do ask them to look*. And these are some of the things which different people report seeing.

The general result of seeing these things is that the person now knows that he or she was not abandoned by God. He or she was not alone. He or she was cared for, and is loved by God. Since this is now an experience which they have had, it is not a vague idea or a mere theological thought. It is a reality that God was there, that He cared, and, often, that He helped. That makes a difference.

A Final Word of Encouragement

None who has made this journey has regretted it. A few have not traveled very far. Those who "had all the answers" when they came were rarely able to get many more. Those who wanted to conduct their own process along to their own lines, and the lines had nothing to do with anything I have laid out, did not seem to get much help from me. Those who were not ready to deal with any discomfort were not able to deal with very much.

The results for those who have tried to work in this way have been very rewarding. One general result of the process as a whole is that the person has more conscious knowledge than they ever had about events that had happened to them, and this may include new knowledge of many more incidents of injury, but none of it now has the pain it once had. They are truly able to forgive. They are truly set free themselves. Physical ailments may disappear. Persons' bodies may physically change, allowing the cancellation of scheduled surgery. Some have reported sleeping well for the first time in decades; others report that voices long active in their minds have been stilled. Many become less anxious. They may become more sociable and more confident and more outgoing. For some, their grooming may improve and become more gender appropriate. Some marriages have been restored. Some are able to do better at work and manage their finances better. They are all generally happier and healthier. They volunteer more. They serve more. They enjoy life more. They may well have pain for a season, sometimes very great pain, as they recall injuries to themselves or embarrassments or disgraces they committed, but on the other side of the process are freedom, release, peace, strength and joy.

Effects have causes. It was a spiritual law before it was a scientific one. Sometimes the causes are spiritual. Sometimes the causes are not readily apparent. If you experience things in life which you find to be disorders, it might be wise to look for causes. God can help you find them. Sometimes it helps to have a trustworthy friend on this quest. When you find a cause, especially if it has been hidden, or a cause of which you were not previously aware, there are a series of things to do which God has given us in the Bible which I think you will find healing.

You may try to do these things outside of a relationship with Christ, and you may very well receive some benefit. However, you will receive more benefit and with more certainty and with more security if you have a relationship with Jesus Christ, therefore, I highly recommend that you ask Jesus Christ to be your Lord and Savior. When God has shown you an issue to work with, then do these things: Mourn it, which means to tell God how wrong it was and how much it hurt. Forgive the perpetrators, which means especially to surrender vengeance to God; turn them over to Him. Repent, which means to commit to turn away from all wrong, especially from any wrong related to the specific injury being worked through. Renew your mind, which means to let God replace the lies you have believed with his truth. Ask Jesus to heal you. Then if you wish, ask God to reveal to you his presence for your care even in the midst of the trauma.

If you are helping another, be gentle. If you are readily filled with self-righteous indignation, then you are not ready to help; don't try; you probably need help yourself. If people are coming to you for help, then they are more like the ones who came to Jesus for help and not like the Pharisees and the Sadducees who came to Jesus to trip him up. Jesus *never* beat up on the honest seeker. Don't you. We need both the truth and the grace that the disciples saw in Jesus [John 1:14], both, not one or the other. Paul tells us that we are to speak the truth in love [Ephesians 4:15]. If you cannot speak in love, do not offer yourself as a helper. If people are entrusting you with their deepest hurts, fears and embarrassments, that is a profound privilege. If you cannot treat their trust as such, do not accept their trust. If you can, and you rely on God, and, I think, if you use the principles I have outlined above, you should have the joy of being an agent of great freedom for many people. May it be so.

If you are seeking help, I pray God empower you to use these principles in a way that helps to set you free. If you need someone to help you through this work, and that may well be the case, then may God lead you to an able and gracious person of God to help you on this journey. There may be pain for a season, but the birth of a new person is well worth it. The other side of the journey is freedom, release, joy, love and peace. Go for it. God wants us well, healthy, sound, and whole. He came that we may have abundant life [John 10:10], to set the captives free [Luke 4:18], and to lighten your burdens [Matthew 11:28]. Don't settle for any less. He will be with you in this work [Matthew 28:20, Philippians 1:6 and 2:12-13]. It may be difficult, but in Him you can do it [John 16:33], for He has overcome the world.

God go with you. God bless you. Go with God.

JIM HILL

About the Author:

Pastor Jim Hill has been the pastor of the North Clairemont United Methodist Church in San Diego, California, for the last sixteen years. He was for many years the President of the Evangelical Fellowship for Church Renewal in the California-Pacific Annual Conference. From 1994 to 2000, he was President of the Board of Transforming Congregations, a national United Methodist ministry to persons in sexual brokenness. He was formerly the President of the Board Frazee Community Center, a multi-site United Methodist social service agency in San Bernardino County. He was formerly President of The Highland Council on Aging, Highland Senior Center, in Highland, California. He formerly served on the Board of Care House, an interdenominational ministry to women with a crisis pregnancy, in San Diego, California. He has served for two different periods on the Conference Board of Evangelism of the California-Pacific Annual Conference

Pastor Hill wrote a series of articles on ministry to the homeless in *Southern California Christian Times*, in

1999-2000. He has been published in the *American Journal of Pastoral Counseling*, and he has chapters in *Pastoral Care and Counseling in Sexual Diversity* edited by H. Newton Malony, and in *Staying the Course: Supporting the Church's Position on Homosexuality*, edited by Maxie Dunnam and H. Newton Malony. He is the author of *The Drinks Are on the Kingdom: The Wedding at Cana and the Kingdom of God* and *To Be Made Whole: A Handbook for Inner Healing*, both published by Vision Publishing. Pastor Hill has been a guest lecturer at UCLA, USD, and at the Fuller School of Theology's School of Psychology. He has also spoken at various churches and conferences.

Pastor Hill has studied at Occidental College, UCLA, School of Theology at Claremont, and at Fuller Theological Seminary. He has a BA in history (67) and an MA in East Asian History (68) both from UCLA, and an MDiv (85) from Fuller.

www.ingramcontent.com/pod-product-compliance
Lightning Source LLC
Chambersburg PA
CBHW071704090426
42738CB00009B/1653